Cameroon

Sean Sheehan and Josie Elias

mc Marshall Cavendish
Benchmark

PICTURE CREDITS

Cover: © imagebroker / Alamy
AFP/Getty Images: 9, 24, 25 • Alexa Stankovic/AFP/Getty Images: 110 •Anthony Ham/Lonely Planet Images:
81 • Audrius Tomonis: 135 • Hutchison Library: 15, 16, 17, 22, 31, 60, 62, 68, 79, 93, 94, 97, 98, 99, 100, 107,
111, 115, 118, 119, 120, 123, 124, 126 • Issouf Sanogo/AFP/Getty Images: 29, 34 • Jason Laure: 14, 26, 47, 65
Martin Van Der Belen/AFP/Getty Images: 37 • Michael Nichols/National Geographic Society Images: 8 •
Northwind Picture Archives: 21 • Photolibrary: 1, 3, 5, 6, 7, 12, 18, 30, 38, 39, 40, 41, 42, 43, 46, 48, 50, 51, 52,
54, 55, 56, 58, 61, 63, 64, 66, 67, 70, 71, 72, 75, 76, 77, 80, 84, 85, 86, 88, 89, 90, 91, 92, 96, 102, 103, 104, 108,
109, 114, 116, 117, 122, 129, 130, 131 • Three Lions/Hulton Archive/Getty Images: 23 • Topfoto: 10 • Topham
Picturepoint: 27, 74, 125, 128 • Trip Photographic Agency: 10, 13, 20, 36, 45, 59, 73, 83, 113

PRECEDING PAGE
A young Cameroonian girl smiling shyly at the camera.

Publisher (U.S.): Michelle Bisson
Editors: Deborah Grahame-Smith, Stephanie Pee
Copyreader: Daphne Hougham
Designers: Nancy Sabato, Steven Tan
Cover picture researcher: Connie Gardner
Picture researchers: Thomas Khoo, Joshua Ang

Marshall Cavendish Benchmark
99 White Plains Road
Tarrytown, NY 10591
Website: www.marshallcavendish.us

© Times Media Private Limited 1999
© Marshall Cavendish International (Asia) Private Limited 2011
® "Cultures of the World" is a registered trademark of Times Publishing Limited.

Originated and designed by Times Media Private Limited
An imprint of Marshall Cavendish International (Asia) Private Limited
A member of Times Publishing Limited

Marshall Cavendish is a trademark of Times Publishing Limited.

Library of Congress Cataloging-in-Publication Data
Sheehan, Sean, 1951-
  Cameroon / Sean Sheehan and Josie Elias. — [2nd ed.].
    p. cm. — (Cultures of the world)
  Includes bibliographical references and index.
  Summary: "Provides comprehensive information on the geography, history,
wildlife, governmental structure, economy, cultural diversity, peoples,
religion, and culture of Cameroon"—Provided by publisher.
  ISBN 978-1-60870-214-5
  1. Cameroon—Juvenile literature. I. Elias, Josie. II. Title.
DT564.S48 2011
967.11--dc22   2010019623

Printed in China
7 6 5 4 3 2 1

CONTENTS

INTRODUCTION

THE REPUBLIC OF CAMEROON LIES IN EQUATORIAL, TROPICAL, central-west Africa. It is a Central African nation on the Gulf of Guinea. Stretching inland from its short Atlantic coastline to the heart of the African continent, its territory includes a portion of Lake Chad in the northeast. Its area is 184,000 square miles (475,440 square kilometers), slightly larger than the state of California. The present country was formed in 1961 when the former French Cameroon and a part of British Cameroon merged. In this land of mountains, grasslands, and forests live an astonishing variety of cultural groups, numbering over 200, who are gradually casting off a colonial heritage acquired in long periods of foreign rule by France and Britain. Cameroon has generally enjoyed stability, which has permitted the development of roads, railways, and agriculture, as well as a petroleum industry. It is one of the few countries in Africa that has managed to evolve from a colony to an independent nation with very little bloodshed and is maturing both economically and politically despite inevitable challenges.

GEOGRAPHY

The volcanic plugs of Rumsiki.

CHAPTER 1

CAMEROON SHARES ITS BORDERS with a number of other countries: Nigeria to the northwest, Chad to the northeast, the Central African Republic to the east, and Equatorial Guinea, Gabon, and Congo to the south.

Cameroon is not landlocked; it is bordered by the Atlantic Ocean to the southwest, and Lake Chad forms part of its northernmost frontier.

FOUR REGIONS

Cameroon has four main geographical regions: the Chad basin, the central plateaus, the western highlands, and the coastal lowlands.

A small boat on the Chari River, the border between Chad and Cameroon.

The climate of Cameroon varies from tropical along the coast to semiarid and hot in the north. The terrain is coastal plain in the southwest, dissected plateau in the center, plains in the north, and mountains in the west. Mount Cameroon, an active volcano, is the highest mountain in sub-Saharan West Africa. Throughout the country several areas of thermal springs tell of prior or current volcanic activity.

The Sangha River forms the border between Cameroon and the Democratic Republic of the Congo.

The Chad basin, located at the northern tip of Cameroon, depends on the Logone River and its rich fishing grounds, which provide the main source of food for the people living in the area. The Logone River flows for 240 miles (386 km) northwest to N'Djamena and Chad, then combines with the Chari River.

The most important feature of north-central Cameroon is the volcanic upland of the grassy, rugged Adamawa Plateau, which extends into southeastern Nigeria. The plateau forms the main watershed of Cameroon and has a major influence on the country's weather patterns. It was named after Modibo Adama, a 19th-century Fulani scholar and warrior who founded a state in the area. From the plateau, which has an average elevation of 3,600 feet (1,097 meters), a number of major rivers flow into Lake Chad, the Congo Basin, the Gulf of Guinea, and the Niger River in Nigeria. The most important of these rivers is the Bénoué (Benue), a 673-mile-long (1,083-km) tributary of the Niger River. The Bénoué descends more than 2,000 feet

LAKE NYOS DISASTER

In the evening of August 21, 1986, there was a mysterious eruption of a large amount of carbon dioxide gas (around 0.240 cubic miles or 1 cubic km) from Lake Nyos (also spelled Nios) in the mountainous region of western Cameroon near the Nigerian border. The gas—which is odorless, colorless, and heavier than oxygen—flowed downhill from the lake and enveloped a number of helpless small villages along the valley. Due to its weight, the gas displaced the oxygen in the air, and 1,746 people and a large number of livestock suffocated as a result. The scientific explanation for this phenomenon is that some kind of volcanic activity below the earth's surface triggered the release of the gas from the water in which it was pocketed.

Much of the Bénoué River flows through the Bénoué National Park, known for its abundant wildlife.

(610 m) over many rapids. Along the northeastern border, the Logone joins the Chari River, which empties into Lake Chad. There are a number of lower plateaus toward the south. The steep falls of some of the rivers, as they flow to the coast, have been exploited to produce hydroelectric power.

The western highlands, sometimes called the Cameroon highlands or the grasslands, is an area with volcanic activity, though today the only volcano that is still active is Mount Cameroon, actually the sole major mountain in West Africa. In the highlands there are numerous volcanic lakes. In 1986 Lake Nyos—a volcanic crater lake—released a noxious gas that was blamed for the deaths of 1,746 people.

The coastal lowlands are characterized by numerous rivers that form swampy areas as they break up into small streams. This terrain provides ideal conditions for mangrove trees, which flourish along parts of the coast.

Many people still live, work, and play near the foot of Mount Cameroon, despite its occasional volcanic eruptions.

MOUNT CAMEROON

Fako is the highest point on Mount Cameroon (Mont Cameroun in French), standing at a height of 13,435 feet (4,095 m), and it is situated 14 miles (23 km) inland from the Gulf of Guinea. Mount Cameroon is the highest peak in sub-Saharan western and central Africa. The port of Limbé, formerly called Victoria, lies at the southern foot of the mountain. The seaward side of the mountain has the reputation of being one of the wettest parts of Cameroon, where more than 394 inches (1,000 cm) of rain falls a year. In 1861 the English explorer Sir Richard Francis Burton (1821—90) was the first European to climb to the top. Still active, volcanic Mount Cameroon last erupted in 2000.

The lush rain forest at Korup National Park safeguards countless hardwoods.

CLIMATE

For an equatorial country, Cameroon has a surprisingly variable climate. This is due to a number of local factors affecting weather patterns, although Cameroon has a largely tropical climate. The main seasons are not summer and winter but wet and dry periods. Around Douala on the coast, the rainy period often lasts eight wet months. This area has over 169 inches (429 cm) of rain a year. In the Chad basin the wet season lasts only a couple of months, and annual rainfall there is only 100 inches (254 cm).

Altitude affects the temperature, so there can be sizable differences in average temperatures even within the same area. Coastal regions with an altitude of 2,954 feet (900 m) record average temperatures of 70°F (21°C), whereas Douala, which is at sea level, has an average of 79°F (26°C).

The Harmattan, a dry, hot wind that blows from the Sahara during the dry months, also affects the climate. The wind carries with it sand and dust from the desert, adding to the aridity; thus the north of the country, which is nearer to the Sahara, has a longer dry season.

FORESTS AND GRASSLANDS

The combination of different temperatures and rainfall produces two major types of vegetation in Cameroon: equatorial forest and tropical grassland. Rain forest and mangrove swamps are found near the coast, where rainfall is highest. Mangrove trees anchor themselves in swampy water by means of long, spreading roots that reveal their architecture when the tide is out and their complex root system is exposed on the mudbanks. The hardwood rain forest consists of mahogany, ebony, sapelli (or sapele), iroko, and obeche trees. The obeche, or African whitewood, is a large deciduous forest tree that commonly grows up to 200 feet (61 m). Because of the cash value of the hardwood, the rain forests have been aggressively logged.

Moving inland from the coast, annual rainfall decreases and the forest thins out. A mix of forest and grassland then gives way to savanna, where

Waza National Park is home to savanna animals such as lions, monkeys, and white pelicans.

Surrounded by a dense forest, Lake Tison is located about 6 miles (10 km) from Ngaoundéré.

trees and bushes are few. Acacia and baobab trees survive here because they can shed their leaves, prolonging their ability to survive dry periods. There are a few hundred species of acacia trees in Cameroon, and one of them, *Acacia catecu*, produces the dye that was the original source of khaki coloring. The large and impressive-looking baobab tree is distinguished by its massive trunk, part of the tree's water-storage system. A rich variety of grasses grows in Cameroon's savanna belt, the tallest of them reaching over 6 feet (2 m) in height. Evergreen trees and papyrus grass thrive along the riverbanks, benefiting from their close proximity to water.

This variety in vegetation, plus regional factors such as the presence of rich volcanic soil around Mount Cameroon and other parts of the western highlands, accounts for the diverse agricultural potential of the country.

Baby chimpanzees in the Waza National Park are protected Cameroon residents.

FLORA AND FAUNA

Cameroon has a marvelous assortment of flora and fauna. It is widely thought that more and more tourists will visit the country to appreciate the many rare species of plants and animals. Elephants, crocodiles, rhinoceroses, hippopotamuses, lions, panthers, cheetahs, and gorillas are all found in Cameroon, though their numbers are not significant. Less spectacular are tarantulas, also known as palm spiders, which grow as big as saucers. Warthogs—one of the world's endangered animals—still live in the more remote forests. Another rare animal is the drill, a large baboon with a short tail. It has a red lower lip, brown fur, and theatrically colored buttocks.

RESOURCES

Petroleum was discovered in the Gulf of Guinea in the mid-1970s, and crude oil was first produced there in 1977. In 2008, as a result of its developing oil

The flesh and seeds of the African oil palm, yielding edible palm oil and used in making soap and lubricants, is a profitable export item.

fields, crude oil production rose to 81,720 barrels per day (bbl/d), up from 67,000 bbl/d in 2003.

There is tremendous potential for hydroelectric power. Cameroon relies on the existing hydroelectric dams and hydroelectric stations to generate 90 percent of the electricity for its towns and cities.

Limestone and a kind of rock called pozzolana, used in the manufacturing of cement, are found in plentiful supply in Cameroon. The country also benefits from deposits of bauxite, diamonds, and iron ore, but these resources are not yet exploited commercially on a large scale.

CITIES

The placement and development of many towns in Cameroon can be traced back to the country's colonial era. The first Europeans to arrive at the coast of Cameroon were part of a 1472 Portuguese expedition led by Fernando Po.

A tribal settlement already existed on the coast at Douala when the first European traders arrived in this part of West Africa, but it was under German colonial rule that the place developed into the country's largest port.

During their domination, the Germans established a trading station at Yaoundé to lock out their French and British trading rivals. No large villages existed in the Yaoundé area until a fort was built and a telegraph station established. It then developed into an administrative center for trade, and mission schools were set up. Yaoundé grew to become the country's capital city and remains the administrative and educational center, with a population close to 1.677 million (2010 est.).

Douala is the only town in Cameroon with an industrial base, and over three-quarters of the country's industrial activities take place there.

Other important cities include Bamenda, Bafoussam, and Nkongsamba, all located in the more densely populated western part of the country. Most towns in Cameroon are growing rapidly, especially in the west, as many people are migrating to the cities from surrounding rural areas. Since most Cameroonians are not wealthy, the increasing numbers of people moving to urban settings is creating shantytowns where the quality of housing is inadequate and basic facilities such as running water, sanitation, and electricity are in short supply.

Limbé, situated on the coast near the southern foot of Mount Cameroon, is Cameroon's second-largest port. Coffee, cocoa, palm oil, tea, bananas, and rubber are exported through Limbé. Originally christened Victoria, in honor of Queen Victoria of Great Britain, the town was founded in 1858 by Baptist missionaries. Limbé has a population of 84,500 (2001 est.), and its colonial-style architecture is waiting to be discovered by a new generation of tourists.

HISTORY

Detail of the Bandjoun Palace, which is a fine example of traditional Bamiléké architecture and is one of the best preserved structures of the Bamiléké chiefdoms.

L ITTLE IS KNOWN ABOUT THE HISTORY of Cameroon before colonization in the 19th century, partly because the nation did not yet exist as a nation state. Also, until A.D. 1500, none of the great kingdoms that rose to power in West Africa were actually based in what is now Cameroon. Since the country came into existence, its history has been a remarkably stable one.

BEFORE COLONIALISM

Before the 1880s there was no single state covering the area known today as Cameroon. Instead, there were numerous small kingdoms, each of which had its own cultural identity and history. Migration of people between one state and another was common and was usually dictated by shifting patterns of economic relationships. Bantu speakers from equatorial Africa are the first people known to have invaded the south and west of the country. In the 18th and 19th centuries, the Fulani (a pastoral Islamic people of the western Sahel, the semidesert fringe of the Sahara) conquered northern Cameroon.

The first Europeans to navigate down the west coast of Africa as far as the Gulf of Guinea were Portuguese explorers in the late 15th century. In 1472 the first Portuguese ships entered the estuary of the Wouri River and were surprised at the abundance of shrimp in the coastal creeks.

Archaeological evidence discloses that the territory now encompassing Cameroon has been inhabited for at least 50,000 years! There is also evidence that previous kingdoms existed in more recent times. The modern history of Cameroon is dated to 1884 when the German explorer Gustav Nachtigal negotiated protectorate treaties with local chiefs.

A prehistoric fossil stone found in northern Cameroon at the Bénoué National Park.

The name of the river and of the new land were thereupon coined from the Portuguese word for shrimp, *camaroes* (CA-mah-row-es), though it was to be called Camerún by the Spanish, Kamerun by the Germans, Cameroun by the French, and Cameroon by the British.

SLAVE TRADE

In the late 18th century Cameroon and the delta area of the Niger River in Nigeria were the focal points for the embarkation of slaves. An estimated 20,000 men and women left those shores every year, never to return.

As the demand for slaves increased, because of the need for labor on plantations in South, Central, and North America, the trade became big business. Many African traders became rich by organizing large slave-hunting expeditions in the interior.

The slaves were kidnapped or traded inland and then passed along through a string of middlemen until they reached the coast, where European trading ships waited offshore. The slave trade developed a shipping network that was later used for the transportation of commercial goods when the slave trade ended.

GERMAN COLONIALISM

The closing decades of the 19th century witnessed a struggle between European powers for lucrative new colonies in Africa. A growing demand for natural resources in Europe made it profitable for each nation to take

About 12 million Africans were forcibly taken from their land to work as slaves on plantations across the Atlantic Ocean. Many of them died under the brutal trade.

possession of a piece of Africa and treat it as an extension of their own state. This became known as the "scramble for Africa." The Douala people, living around the Wouri River, signed a treaty in July 1884 that permitted German rule in the area close to the river. Palm oil, rubber, tobacco, tea, coffee, bananas, and cocoa were all valuable products worth exporting, so the Germans eventually expanded their domination inland by setting up convenient routes to their plantations. This enterprise brought the colonists into conflict with local traders, who until then had always traded with Europeans on the coast. Violence broke out whenever the locals resisted German incursions.

Although the period of German colonialism lasted only from 1884 to 1916, it was a very decisive period because, for the first time, a boundary was established around the region that would evolve into Cameroon. Mission schools were set up by Germans that eventually produced a small elite group of literate clerks, pastors, and teachers. The Germans also changed the name of their new territory on the west coast of Africa to Kamerun. Douala was developed as the main port, and new settlements were built inland.

A coffee farmer setting off to harvest the beans. Coffee remains as one of the major export crops of Cameroon.

World War I, which broke out in 1914, was partly a struggle between European superpowers to gain control of profitable imperial possessions. Kamerun, a land rich in natural resources, was invaded by French and British armies. When the war ended in 1918 with the defeat of Germany, Kamerun was divided between the victors. Under a League of Nations mandate, the larger share of the territory, about four-fifths of Kamerun, went to France and became French Cameroon. A smaller area in the west that bordered Nigeria went to Great Britain. The country was thus divided into two parts. The British territory was itself split into British Southern Cameroon and British Northern Cameroon.

A SHARED COUNTRY

The British sector was attached to Nigeria, a larger and more valuable part of the British Empire, and many thousands of Nigerians moved into South

Toward the end of their colonial rule, the Germans started segregating Douala into separate white and black areas, as well as forcibly relocating inhabitants. This was an extremely racist act, with a greedy economic motive. The German authorities wanted to acquire the land, which was becoming increasingly valuable, without having to pay local landowners the market price. Resistance to the segregation was organized under the leadership of Rudolph Douala Manga Bell, who was later tried for treason and executed. On the day that he died, in 1914, another rebel, Martin Paul Samba, also faced a firing squad for offering to help the French if they would remove German rule.

Cameroon. In British Cameroon the English language was used in schools and the administration, whereas French was used in the rest of the country. Neither the French nor British imperial power was particularly interested in encouraging their nationals to settle in Cameroon. Their main interest was to exploit the land's economic possibilities by developing plantations, especially for coffee.

A monument to General Philippe Leclerc de Hauteclocque, who led the French colony of Cameroon to join the Free French forces during World War II.

Meanwhile, Douala was growing in importance as a major port, and a small but significant number of industrial companies were set up in the coastal area, including a hydroelectric plant and an aluminum-processing plant. After World War II these developments attracted an even greater number of Europeans to Cameroon. Because European migrants were offered the best employment opportunities, racial tensions began to develop. And a new movement, the sense of nationalism, was spreading among Cameroonians.

NATIONALISM

The influx of Nigerians into British Cameroon, where many of them held minor positions of authority in the police force and the judiciary, led to the feeling that Cameroon was becoming a subcolony of a colony. This strengthened calls from the indigenous peoples for reunification of the two parts of the

Ahmadou Ahidjo, the first president of Cameroon, ruled with a strong arm for 22 years.

country. A labor organization in French Cameroon, l'Union des Populations du Cameroun (UPC), went underground and called for active resistance to French rule. In 1956 a form of self-government was introduced by France. The colonial power remained in control of foreign policy, and a coalition government was established. This government fell from power in 1958, and a second coalition government was formed under the leadership of Ahmadou Ahidjo in 1959. There now were calls for complete independence, and Ahidjo's government offered an amnesty to UPC nationalists, who agreed to cease their guerrilla war against the French administration.

INDEPENDENCE FOR FRENCH CAMEROON

French Cameroon gained independence on January 1, 1960, and the Republic of Cameroon came into existence. It was not generally known at the time, but agreements had been made to preserve French economic and military interests to ensure a peaceful transition to independence.

There was no constitution when Ahmadou Ahidjo became ruler of the country in 1960. He consolidated his own political power and tailored a

Soldiers in a parade at Yaoundé to celebrate Cameroon's independence in 1960.

constitution that suited the interests of the government and the people he represented. New elections took place four months after independence, and although the UPC was allowed to take part, Ahidjo's party, the Union Camerounaise (UC), won 51 of the 100 seats in the parliament. Ahidjo himself ran for election as president and, being the only candidate, was elected. His party sought to avoid open conflict and formed a coalition government with all the parties except the UPC.

COMPLETE INDEPENDENCE

In British Cameroon before 1960 there were appeals for reunification with French Cameroon, but at the same time, there were calls by other groups for a merger with Nigeria. The British rulers gradually allowed greater autonomy to Cameroon representatives in the Nigerian federal government. In 1961 a plebiscite was held, and voters were given the choice between unification

Cameroonians have enjoyed peace and stability since independence in 1960.

with Nigeria or with the new Republic of Cameroon. The result for British Southern Cameroon was overwhelmingly in favor of reunification with the former French Cameroon. British Northern Cameroon chose to join Nigeria. In October 1961 the Federal Republic of Cameroon came into existence, uniting the British Southern and French colonial areas into one new country.

THE AHIDJO YEARS

Ahmadou Ahidjo was the first president of the republic and remained the undisputed leader of Cameroon's government until 1982. He was a dictator, personally commanding nearly all aspects of political life. He began by forming a single political party, the Cameroon National Union (CNU), in the French-influenced eastern part of the country and merging it with a number of different parties in the British-influenced west of the country. Parties failing to cooperate with this process were outlawed and their leaders arrested and imprisoned. In theory it was possible for new political parties to be formed, but in reality it was extremely difficult and no emerging party was allowed to develop an effective voice. Military force was used to destroy the remnants of the UPC opposition to the new state. Labor unions were forced to form a single organization, which then came under the political control of the government.

President Ahidjo with officials at the opening of a new health center.

State power became centralized in Yaoundé, and previous forms of local government were dismantled. In 1972 the federal system of government was abolished and the country became the United Republic of Cameroon. A number of provinces were created, each one overseen by a governor and regional officers. All government officials were appointed by Ahidjo. Cameroon was under a political, not military, dictatorship because Ahidjo was able to use his great power to win cooperation from individuals and groups who might otherwise have mounted opposition to his rule. At the same time, it was generally known that political opposition to Ahidjo would not be tolerated, and civil rights such as press freedom were severely constrained.

Ahidjo's ability to single-handedly rule his country was aided by the financial support of the French government and the commercial backing of his regime that came from the powerful business interests that remained largely under French control. At the grassroots level Ahidjo was able to hand out jobs and contracts to local people who would continue to support him. The civil service went through a process of "Cameroonization," replacing French bureaucrats with Cameroonian ones. This helped to ensure loyalty to the government.

THE BIYA YEARS

President Ahmadou Ahidjo resigned in 1982, handing over the presidency to his prime minister, Paul Biya. A peaceful and voluntary transfer of power in Africa is not a very frequent event, so it was commonly assumed at the time that Ahidjo did not intend to relinquish all his power. But Biya emerged as an independent leader who was not willing to act as a puppet for Ahidjo. In 1983 the resignation of Ahidjo as president of the CNU and his replacement by Biya marked a decisive shift of power. A plot against the Biya government was said to have been uncovered, and rumors circulated that Ahidjo was implicated in this.

Once in power, Paul Biya proclaimed the need for a more democratic form of government. Ahidjo, who left the country and went into exile in France in 1983, was found guilty of involvement in a plot to take over the government and was sentenced to death. Although his sentence was later reduced, it provoked another coup attempt in 1984 in which an estimated 500 to 1,000 people were killed by government forces, and many others were detained or imprisoned before the rebellion was crushed.

Following the coup, Paul Biya obtained 99.98 percent of the votes in a presidential election where he was the only candidate. By 1986 Biya was still not allowing opposition parties to register, but he changed the name of his own party from UNC to Rassemblement Démocratique du Peuple Camerounais (RDPC), probably to distance himself from former-president Ahidjo. In the 1998 presidential election Paul Biya was again the only candidate, and with 98.75 percent of the votes he prevailed for a new term in office.

In May 1990 the Social Democratic Front (SDF) had been formed without permission from the government. A founding rally was held in Bamenda, but although it was intended to be peaceful, riots broke out and six people were killed. A draft for a multiparty system was laid out by the president, and after a few months more than 20 parties had registered, every one of them in strong opposition to Biya's ruling party. Biya dismissed the plans for a multiparty system, banned opposition rallies, and placed seven provinces in Cameroon under military rule.

Cameroonian president Paul Biya was elected in 1992 and reelected in 2004 and 2007.

A campaign for civil disobedience was launched in 1991, and a general strike was called. The strike did not end until the government agreed to support the work of a constitutional committee, which had formed to discuss the political future of Cameroon. Legislative elections took place in 1992 and opposition parties were allowed to run, but Biya did all he could to ensure his reelection, including shutting down all independent newspapers. In the presidential election of 1992, Biya won 39.9 percent of the votes and the opposition leader, John Fru Ndi, got 35.9 percent. Observers from the United States reported election fraud, and a state of emergency was declared in the western provinces. John Fru Ndi and many others were put under house arrest. In the 1997 legislative elections the opposition parties called for a boycott of the undemocratic elections, but the opposition was split, and Biya was reelected. Paul Biya was reelected in 2004 and again in 2007.

GOVERNMENT

The facade of a town hall in Yaoundé.

OVER THE YEARS OF ITS EXISTENCE, Cameroon has had a remarkably stable government, though for much of that time it has been one-party domination.

The first constitution of 1961 was changed in 1972 when the United Republic of Cameroon was formed. Executive powers remained in the hands of the president, who is the head of the government and chief of the armed forces. He also appoints all the ministers. The president is elected for a period of seven years by direct and secret universal suffrage. Legislative power is held by a National Assembly of 180 members, elected for five-year terms. The republic is divided into 10 administrative regions, each headed by a governor. Each region is divided into departments or divisions.

A government office building in the capital of Cameroon, Yaoundé.

Cameroon is a unitary republic supporting a multiparty presidential regime. The Referendum of May 20, 1972, united East Cameroon and West Cameroon, giving birth to the United Republic of Cameroon. The government consists of an executive body ruled by the president. The executive controls the cabinet, the court system, and the legislative body.

STARTING FROM SCRATCH

When Cameroon became an independent state in 1960, there was a need to choose a form of government and to create a constitution. A sense of identity to unite all Cameroonians—over and above the many ethnic loyalties that divided the citizens of the new state—had to be created, too. In particular, people from the British and French areas of influence and people from the northern and southern parts of the country had to be pulled together to live in harmony. Without some sense of shared identity, there loomed a danger that the nation would fall apart.

Many newly emerging African states were confronted with such problems in the 1960s. Many of them, such as Cameroon, had been shaped and defined by colonial experiences that had never nurtured national identity. In many cases, including Cameroon, the physical boundaries of the states had been artificially created by resident colonial powers, and new national territories had forced wildly different ethnic groups together, each with its own language and culture. Such volatile situations gave new governments excuses to create authoritarian political systems.

AHIDJO'S GOVERNMENT

From independence until 1982 Cameroon was governed by Ahmadou Ahidjo. He created a presidential system of government that invested nearly all the powers of state in his own position as the president.

The constitution was altered so that the president became the head of state, the head of government, and the commander in chief of military forces. The National Assembly had been awarded no executive powers at all and simply rubber-stamped whatever legislation the president proposed. Ministers, governors, and judges were all appointed by the president. When elections of the National Assembly took place, the party that received the majority of votes automatically won all the available seats. This made it virtually impossible for any new party to win representation in the assembly because they would have to obtain over 50 percent of all votes in the country. Thus the CNU always remained in power.

AHMADOU AHIDJO

Ahmadou Ahidjo was born in Cameroon in 1924 and died of a heart attack while in exile in France in 1989 after having been sentenced to death for alleged involvement in an antigovernment coup. He served as president for some 22 years, from May 1960 to November 1982, and although he insisted on retaining power strictly for himself and his own party, he kept his country free of the internal power struggles that destabilized other African nations that had gained their independence around the same time. His greatest achievement was overseeing the peaceful and successful emergence of Cameroon as one united nation, formed from two separate and not always harmonious states. A Muslim from northern Cameroon, Ahidjo maintained control and stability with the active support of the French government.

BIYA'S GOVERNMENT

When Paul Biya gained power in 1982, he announced the need for more democracy and changed the constitution to allow non-CNU members to run in presidential elections. Nonetheless, there was still no opposition when Biya won his first full term as president in 1984. The concentration of power in the hands of the president remained intact. What changed were the new president's willingness to use his great power to bring about some relaxation of the dictatorial state's practices and his pledge to introduce democratic reforms.

Important changes appeared in the running of government ministries. People were appointed because of their skill and aptitude for the jobs and not just their political usefulness to the president. In 1987 Biya wrote a book entitled *Communal Liberalism* in which he explained the kind of government he wanted to bring about and the need for the "establishment of a new political society." He also made it clear that although a multiparty state was a goal to aim for, it would be necessary to maintain one-party rule for the time being.

Biya proclaimed the need for a National Charter of Freedom, too, a defined set of human rights that would apply to all Cameroonians. Although press censorship still exists today, it is felt that more freedom is allowed under Biya than ever was possible under Ahidjo.

In 1984 Biya changed the country's name from United Republic of Cameroon to simply the Republic of Cameroon, asserting that the people had become united, and so there was no longer a need for the word "United."

NEW PARTIES

Cameroon was a one-party state from 1966 and was dominated by the CNU. In March 1985 the CNU became the Cameroon People's Democratic Movement (CPDM) or RDPC. The change of name was not enough to persuade people that the governing party was interested in serious democratic reforms, and the second half of the 1980s witnessed political unrest and violent clashes between government forces and groups demanding political change. In 1990

Presidential candidate Ni John Fru Ndi at a campaign rally in 2004, speaking for the opposition party Front Social Démocrate.

a constitutional amendment established a multiparty system, although the RDPC remained dominant. Other constitutional reforms in 1993 sought to decentralize the government. The main opposition was the SDF (also known in French as Front Social Démocrate, FSD), which challenged Biya for the presidency.

THE JUDICIARY

Cameroon has a Higher Judicial Council that is constitutionally responsible, together with the president, for guaranteeing the independence of the judiciary and the equality of all citizens before the law. The role of the council is to advise the president on the nomination of magistrates and judges and to monitor the performance of their duties.

The Cameroonian legal system as well as the sources of law applicable in the country have been shaped and influenced by the dual English-French colonial heritage. This has been described as bijural, consisting of two legal systems, English Common Law and French Civil Law. This makes Cameroon one of the few examples of a dual legal system in the world. French civil law applies in the eight French-speaking regions, and English law applies in the two English-speaking regions. In precolonial Cameroon there existed traditional or customary law. This included Muslim law that was already in place in the northern part of the country. The British and the French both recognized and enforced customary law to a degree, generally only if it were not considered repugnant to natural justice, equity, and good conscience, and if it did not conflict with any existing French or English law.

The legal system of Cameroon consists of the supreme court, two courts of appeal, high courts, and circuit courts. The supreme court has the power to decide whether a bill should be taken before the National Assembly when a disagreement between the president and the legislature arises. There is also a court of impeachment that can judge the president in cases of high treason and on other government ministers in the event of a coup against the government.

The beautifully painted walls of a village chief's house. In rural areas the house of a chief is usually larger than that of anyone else.

CHIEFS

In precolonial times, the power of government operated through a system of chiefs. Each chief or *fon* (FON) had his own special hut and, depending on local political arrangements, had a number of more powerful chiefs he was subservient to and smaller chiefs that he could rule. The chief combined the powers of judge and jury for his own village, leading to the view that the chief was an autocratic ruler with dictatorial powers. This was not true, however, in most cases. Many chiefs governed with the input of a council of older and more respected members of the community. This modifying force tempered the chiefs' unilateral powers.

Chiefs today no longer wield any official political power, although it is not uncommon for a chief to hold a local government post. Official or not, the chiefs still exercise significant social influence as pillars of tradition and continuity.

INTERNATIONALISM

Cameroon has a long-standing and important relationship with France, since a sizable part of the country used to be a French colony. At the time of independence, France played an important role in shaping the government that emerged in Cameroon, and it still maintains an influence in the land it once controlled. The two countries have economic, diplomatic, military, and cultural links, and together they strengthen and preserve a relationship that was forged in the era of colonialism. Critics sometimes argue that Cameroon is still too closely tied to its old colonial master, because the economic and military links encourage a relationship of dependency. Nevertheless, Cameroon has developed friendly relations, both economic and diplomatic, with other nations both within and outside of Europe. Cameroon's historical ties to Great Britain account for its continuing membership in the Commonwealth of Nations.

RECENT ELECTIONS

Paul Biya, representing the RDPC, won another term of office as president in the October 1997 presidential election, receiving over 92 percent of the 4 million votes cast. Elections for the National Assembly had taken place in May 1997, in which the RDPC won 116 of the 180 seats. The SDF won 43 seats; the National Union for Democracy and Progress (UNDP, Union Nationale pour la Démocratie et le Progrès) won 13 seats; the Cameroon Democratic Union (Union Démocratique du Cameroun, UDC) won 5 seats; and 3 seats were won by independent candidates (others). Meanwhile, because of opposition forces's allegations of vote rigging, backed by international observers' reports by the opposition forces, the supreme court annulled the result of three constituencies (7 seats). Peter Mafany, a longtime supporter of Biya, was active head of the Cameroon government from September 19, 1996.

A woman casting her vote during polling for municipal and legislative elections in 2007.

After a cabinet reshuffle, Biya was elected to a further term of office in the October 2004 presidential elections, this time winning 70.92 percent of the votes. Ni John Fru Ndi, representing the SDF, won 17.4 percent of the votes; Dr. Adamou Ndam Njoya, representing the UDC, won 4.48 percent; Garga Haman Adji of the Alliance for Democracy and Development (Alliance pour la Démocratie et le Développement, ADD) won 3.74 percent of the votes; and smaller parties won the remaining 3.46 percent.

In the National Assembly elections of 2007, the RDPC won 153 of the 180 seats. The SDF won 16 seats, the UNDP won 6 seats, the UDC won 4 seats, and the Progressive Movement (MP) won 1 seat.

ECONOMY

A Cameroonian woman preparing fabric for
batik dyeing.

>C AMEROON IS PROUD THAT THE country has enough resources to feed its people. Self-sufficiency in food distinguishes it from many other African states. Cameroon also has an enviable reputation for economic stability, and its market-oriented policies attract foreign investment.

Its economy accounts for half the gross domestic product (GDP) of all the countries of Central Africa combined. On the downside, the

A vendor packaging charcoal to sell at the local market.

After gaining its independence, Cameroon saw its economy swing from a period of prosperity to a decade of recession, followed by partial recovery. Cameroon's favorable geographic position, wealth of natural resources, and relative political stability have together allowed Cameroon to build one of the most diverse and prosperous economies in sub-Saharan Africa.

realization of a free market has produced problems such as corruption and the destruction of Cameroon's old forests for short-term gain. For much of the 1990s there was no economic growth, and the country's reliance on the World Bank and the International Monetary Fund (IMF) meant that its economic policies were largely driven by these institutions. This explains the government's policy of privatizing many sectors of the economy. Tax laws have been revised and reforms undertaken to encourage investment. Moreover, several infrastructure projects have been launched that should energize business expectations.

AGRICULTURE

Three out of four Cameroonians live and work on their own land, producing around 90 percent of the country's food. The national economy is heavily dependent on agriculture. In 2009 agriculture contributed 19.8 percent to the

A thriving banana plantation near Mount Kupe. Bananas are wrapped in blue plastic to protect them from pests.

Workers packing cotton for export at a depot in southern Cameroon.

GDP. The average size of a farmstead is small, around 7 acres (3 hectares), but this is adequate to maintain a lifestyle that is reasonably self-sufficient. Cash crops include coffee, bananas, peanuts, palm oil, palm kernels or seeds, cotton, rubber, and cocoa from cacao beans.

In the north farmers primarily grow grain and raise animals. In the south there is more agricultural variety: millet, rice, bananas, peanuts (which are called groundnuts), corn, and cassava are grown, and cattle, goats, sheep, and horses are raised. Lake Chad and the rivers flowing into it provide a rich supply of fish. On the plateaus farther south, the conditions are suitable for growing cotton, cacao, coffee, and tobacco. Cameroon is among the world's largest producers of cocoa; 300,000 tons of cacao beans were produced in 2006. The altitude and climate of the western highlands is ideal for planting coffee, corn, peanuts, bananas, and plantains. The forested area in the south, which is not suitable for cattle, produces sorghum, sweet potatoes, and yams, as well as more cacao than any other region.

Logging in the old forest of Eschiembot. Beautiful woods are always in demand.

TRADE

Colonial footprints are seen in most aspects of Cameroonian life, and the economy is no exception. When the country gained independence, around 60 percent of exports went to France. This has gradually dropped to 25 percent in recent years. Although Cameroon has developed trading ties with other countries, France still supplies almost half of its total imports. Other important trading partners are Italy, Spain, Holland, Germany, Japan, Great Britain, and the United States. Also, trade with other African and Arab countries has increased.

Cameroon's major exports are crude oil and petroleum products, coffee, cacao beans, cotton, tea, rubber, peanuts, bananas, aluminum, and timber. Imports consist mainly of industrial and household goods, motor vehicles and other transportation equipment, as well as spare parts, fertilizers, and pesticides.

Cameroon is on its way to becoming a capitalist state operating on the basis of private enterprise and the free flow of capital, although the majority of its citizens still practice subsistence farming. Many new businesses have sprouted over the years.

FOREST DESTRUCTION

Cameroon produces more cut trees for lumber than any country in Africa, and this has resulted in very few virgin forests remaining. Even though Cameroon still has one of the largest tropical forests on the continent, this rampant harvesting has depressing consequences for the environment and wildlife of the region. Forestry experts believe that Cameroon is exploiting this resource at a faster rate than it can sustain through replanting, and the long-term result will be the total destruction of a valuable and beautiful resource.

Part of the problem arises from governmental concessions sold to private companies to exploit an area of forest. In addition, the prevalence

Deforestation on and around Mount Oku in the Bamenda Highlands. Irresponsible logging and agricultural practices have contributed to the decrease of forests in Cameroon.

A commercial company engrossed in maximizing its profits does not look at a forest with the same eyes as a conservation group. Conservationists regard the forest as a whole, seeking to preserve its ecological identity, and they understand that any one area of a forest contains different types of trees growing in harmony. From a narrow commercial point of view, it makes sense to select and log only the most valuable trees in an area. It has been estimated, however, that 10 percent of a forest area is sacrificed in the process of getting to and removing a single selected high-value tree. In this way, over a period of time, the entire forest will be seriously damaged, even though only relatively few trees will have actually been cut down. Cameroon has one of the highest deforestation rates in Africa, losing some 543,600 acres (220,000 ha) or 850 square miles (2,200 square km) of forest per year. Building access roads into previously dense forest encourages illegal hunters to poach because their activities become a lot easier. Antelope, chimpanzees, and gorillas are hunted down and shot for sale as "bushmeat" in the local towns.

of corruption is poorly controlled in Cameroon, and this means that the more unscrupulous companies—the ones that pay the fattest bribes—are often more likely to obtain logging contracts. This tends to sideline the environmentally responsible companies, leaving corrupt ones with opportunities to abuse their position by excessive logging, disregarding replanting and conservation.

TOURISM

Tourists are attracted to African states because of the opportunities to see exotic wildlife and to experience novel and dramatic landscapes. Cameroon is able to tap into this tourist market because it possesses two important assets. First, Cameroon has an astonishingly rich ecology, ranging from rain forest to rolling savanna—and that includes the most varied flora and fauna in all of Africa. A second asset is the country's economic and political

Tourists find it fascinating to regard village life close-up.

stability, a status that makes tourists feel safer in Cameroon than in some of the neighboring states.

Eight national parks are open to foreign visitors, and because such tours tend to be expensive, they generate high revenue from a relatively small number of visitors. One of the most well-established and successful destinations is Waza National Park, where elephants, antelope, giraffes, lions, and monkeys roam freely. Approximately 185,00 tourists visited Cameroon in 2008.

OPENING MARKETS

Cameroon aims to develop a free-market economic system while still maintaining a political system that is highly centralized and in firm control of the national economy. This is often felt to be a difficult challenge because a highly centralized government that seeks to maintain political control may come in conflict with competing interests of economic groups. The Biya

A container port at Douala, Cameroon's gateway to the world.

government has had mixed success in managing the economy and controlling the state. One advantage of strong state power is the government's ability to offer assurances to foreign companies that their investments will not vaporize in sudden political upheavals. Foreign companies benefit from knowing that their investments will not be nationalized, and this reassurance has enabled Cameroon to attract foreign investment.

As in many African countries, small adverse changes in economic health seriously affect the chances of acquiring the foreign investment essential to finance large-scale ventures. After a downturn in the economy in the mid-1980s, the World Bank was brought in to provide assistance. The Bank's first move was to insist on cuts in government spending. In late 2000 the IMF announced that Cameroon would qualify for the Heavily Indebted Poor Countries (HIPC) debt relief initiative. Moreover, to cover debt service payments, $100 million would be provided annually.

In recent years the government has started to relax some of its grip on the economy. State-owned industries, such as the agency that controls the production of palm oil, are being sold to private companies, and plans are afoot to privatize the cotton industry. Attempts like this to liberalize the economy and encourage private ownership are encouraged by the IMF. Meanwhile, increased oil revenues have helped to reduce the government's debt burden.

OPENING ACCESS

Improvement of the country's roads and transportation network plays a major role in supporting new economic ventures and increasing the investment appeal of Cameroon to foreign banks. Poor roads and heavy rainfall in the south have been largely responsible for shortcomings in the transportation system, somewhat explaining why the north customarily has been isolated from the south. During 2000 and 2004 the Chad-Cameroon Development project invested $3.7 billion to build oil production facilities in southern Chad, a pipeline across Cameroon, and associated infrastructure in both countries. Cameroon's road system is only partially developed, and many rural roads are eroded and poorly maintained. In recent years over 500 miles (800 km) of roads were paved to improve transportation links with Chad and the Central African Republic. Furthermore, the government has prepared a 15-year plan to pave an additional 1,865 miles (3,000 km) of roads.

Most of the industry and workers' quarters in Douala are located on the far end of the Wouri Bridge, on the right bank of the Wouri River.

Douala, on the estuary of the Wouri River, is the country's main port and accounts for nearly all of Cameroon's shipping trade. Douala also handles shipping trade for Chad and the Central African Republic, using the region's wide network of rivers for transportation to and from these neighboring countries. Minor ports include Limbé; Kribi, which transports logs and cacao from the interior; and Tiko, which services the export of bananas, wood, and rubber. In the north, traders in the port of Garoua—on the banks of the Bénoué River—transport goods to Nigeria.

There is an international airport at Yaoundé, but Cameroon Airlines ceased flight operations in 2008. A new national airline, Cameroon Airways Corporation—Camair Co—was structured and organized to replace the country's bankrupt Cameroon Airlines. Helped by Lufthansa Consulting, this enterprise will allow the country's crippled airline industry to take off afresh. Yaoundé, Douala, and Garoua handle local flights, and the number of airports in the interior, for example at Tiko, Ngaoundéré, Bafoussam, Bamenda, and Maroua has been steadily increasing.

ENVIRONMENT

The lush forest canopy at Korup
National Park.

>N ATIONAL PARKS AND PROTECTED areas of Cameroon cover about 4.4 percent of the country. That is equivalent to about 4.9 million acres (2 million ha). Even within reserved forests, destruction is heavy. Fires and commercial exploitation of the forests result in the annual loss of 200,000 acres (80,940 ha).

Additionally, the semiarid northern rangelands are being overgrazed, and by the mid-1980s Cameroon had lost an estimated 40 percent of its mangrove swamps. Air pollution caused by industrial chemicals and vehicle emissions is a significant environmental problem. Overfishing and poaching threaten the wildlife, and safe drinking water is also a concern. Volcanic activity, flooding, and insect infestations also cause problems. In 1986 Lake Nyos, which lies within the crater of a dormant volcano, emitted a great bubble of poisonous gas that killed over 1,746 people, and the possibility of a recurrence of this must be addressed.

NATIONAL PARKS AND RESERVES

The national parks and reserves in Cameroon have been developed to provide large safe areas for wildlife and to preserve the flora of the region. They are perfect places to observe wildlife in its natural habitats and have become favored tourist destinations.

In 1986 Korup National Park was established. This area is in Cameroon's Southwest Province, adjacent to the international

A herd of elephants basking in the safety of Waza National Park.

boundary with Nigeria. Previously this area had been designated a forest reserve. Korup contains the widest variety of tree species in any rain forest in Africa. The area receives a great deal of rainfall and relatively little sunshine, and this, combined with poor accessibility, has allowed the natural rain forest to flourish. The park contains the plant *Ancistrocladus korupensis* (family *Ancistrocladaceae*)—one of the two plants identified by the U.S. National Cancer Institute that can be used to formulate medicines against the human immunodeficiency virus (HIV) that causes acquired immunodeficiency syndrome (AIDS). If the potential of the plant becomes confirmed, it could make a great contribution toward world health.

Korup National Park is one of the largest projects undertaken by the World Wide Fund for Nature, also known as the World Wildlife Fund (WWF). Its mission is to maintain and protect the park while also integrating it into regional development plans. The WWF project includes the Korup National Park and the forest reserves of Nta-Ali, Rumpi Hills, and Ejagham, all together covering an area of 1,737 square miles (4,500 square km). Boundaries are clearly defined and buffer zones have been created for agriculture, watershed protection, and hunting. To encourage tourism without damaging the fragile ecosystem, nature trails have been created and surveillance posts and campsites established. Poaching is strictly forbidden.

There are 29 villages within the Korup area, 6 of them inside the park. Because the lives of the local inhabitants are so intricately interwoven with the forest, they have been educated about wildlife and forest care, trained in local technical colleges, taught regional handicrafts, provided with fertile land outside the park for family farming, and employed as park guards.

These measures reduce poverty and stop the villagers from hunting animals indiscriminately, possibly killing endangered species. The project has been encouraging because many weapons—previously used by the villagers in hunting—have been handed over to the authorities.

The Waza National Park of Cameroon is home to antelope, giraffes, ostriches, gazelles, lions, and elephants, as well as many different birds. It is open to the public for around six months a year, but every vehicle that enters the park must have an official guide. There is nowhere to camp within the park, but visitors may park near the entrance or at the village of Waza.

The Bénoué National Park covers an area of 444,790 acres (180,000 ha). The Bénoué River—habitat of large numbers of hippopotamus colonies—flows for a long while on the park's eastern border. It also has large numbers of elephants, lions, warthogs, waterbuck antelopes, monkeys, and crocodiles. Boubandjidda National Park lies in a remote 543,632-acre (220,000-ha) area on the border with Chad. There flourish antelope, black rhinoceroses, and lions. Dinosaur fossils can also be found in this park. The Dja Faunal Reserve,

Giraffes having a tall drink at **Waza National Park.**

Rising rain forest mist on the slopes of Mount Cameroon.

covering 1,299,774 acres (526,000 ha), is one of the best protected rain forest areas in Africa and is located in the south-central part of the country. The terrain encompasses evergreen and semievergreen forests. Conservation of great apes in this reserve is a prime concern. There are some 107 mammal species, of which 5 are threatened. It is home to about 310 bird species, and the largest breeding colony of grey-necked rockfowl (*Picathartes oreas*) in the whole country. Although this bird inhabits a large range throughout Central Africa, its population is small and fragmented, primarily because of the harvesting and degradation of its habitat.

Cameroon created a new park in 2009, Deng Deng National Park, specifically to protect a population of 600 gorillas and other threatened species such as chimpanzees, forest elephants, buffalo, and bongos. The park spreads over 224 square miles (580 square km), an area approximately the size of Chicago. Takamanda National Park was also created in 2009. Takamanda forms part of a transborder protected area with Nigeria's Cross River National Park and has been established especially to protect the world's rarest gorilla, the Cross River gorilla.

MOUNT CAMEROON Mount Cameroon's designation as a national park in 2010 is expected to bring benefits to the local population as well as conserve the environment. Almost 60 traditional chiefs from around the area gathered in February to sanctify the new venture. Elephants and chimpanzees roam the forests there, and many species of rare plants thrive. People benefit from the resources found on Mount Cameroon, but the human presence puts the entire ecosystem at risk. Poaching and the steady encroachment of towns have placed the animals at risk of extinction. The urbanization of the area has also meant that the water resources are in jeopardy. Farming and agriculture threatens the ecosystem on Mount Cameroon. Trees and brush are cut down and used as firewood. The soil is very fertile and suited to growing crops, but

This program was established at the Rio de Janeiro Earth Summit in 1992. It is a living experiment in the coexistence of human beings and the natural environment, and it is being administered in the Korup National Park area. It is a nongovernmental organization (NGO), but it receives support from a number of governments, including the United States and France. Its mission is to make a contribution to the development and conservation of biological resources. The organization is particularly interested in the use of rain forest plants in medicine. The program is also supported by the French pharmaceutical company Plantecam, which manufactures diverse medical products from natural resources and farms selected plants with the view of aiding conservation of their species.

converting some of the land into an agricultural cooperative has meant that in many places it is now overfarmed and has lost its natural fertility. With its designation as a national park, the government has created investment opportunities in the area, particularly in roads and infrastructure. The park is expected to become an active tourist destination, thereby providing the local jobs necessary to keep the park operational.

DEFORESTATION

Cameroon has one of the highest deforestation rates in Africa, losing some 543,632 acres (220,000 ha) of forest per year, mostly to logging and agriculture. Of the different tree species found in the Mount Cameroon region, *Prunus africana*, or red stinkwood, is the most valuable because of its medicinal value. Locally it is used to treat chest pain, malaria, and even mental illness. Its bark contains active biochemicals used in the treatment of prostate gland disorders. As the current demand for this healing tree is greater than its supply, people need to use the trees prudently. Moreover, many trees are dying due to the poor harvesting methods found in large-scale commercialization.

A traditional healer picking leaves that are thought to be of medicinal value. Many trees and plants that locals depend on economically are being felled greedily.

Unsustainable logging practices also lead to deforestation and forest degradation. Present-day logging practices are imprudent, because extracting 1.3 cubic yards (1 cubic m) of wood inflicts damage to more than 2.6 cubic additional yards (2 cubic m). There is flagrant wastage of wood at the logging sites in the forest, and there is still more wastage at the sawmills, often located at remote areas that are hard to police. It has been estimated that 25 percent of raw logs are wasted!

Developmental projects such as the construction of roads—even the roads that are cut to access a forest—also lead to deforestation. Contour maps essential in the planning of road construction and bridge alignment may not be available. Topographical maps and maps detailing species in the targeted area of forest to be logged may not ever have been made. Logging thus can take place in an area where it is too hard to haul the cut logs to a sawmill or where many trees are indiscriminately destroyed in an effort to get to the tree species that an operator wants to harvest.

Population growth is a significant cause of deforestation and forest degradation. Rural-to-urban migration has been increasing. Population

The smoldering remains of trees and grass razed and burned to clear land for agriculture.

growth has kept pace with food production, so the total area under cultivation has increased proportionately. This has been achieved through the slash-and-burn system of farming that involves clearing a plot by chopping down and burning the trees and underbrush, planting crops such as corn, cocoyams (taro), cassava, and other vegetables for a number of years, and then leaving the plot fallow (unseeded) when the productivity of the soil has been exhausted. Land may be left fallow for more than a dozen years. The farmer simply starts the process somewhere else. This is called shifting cultivation.

Deforestation is also caused by poorly defined property rights. Most logging takes place on communal land that is administered by the state on behalf of the local community. The people have the right to produce on the land, but resources such as trees belong to the state. As a result the people do not have the incentive to manage the land properly. The communities come into conflict with the logging companies when trees—which provide fruit, oils, food, or medicinal materials—are felled to provide milled wood or are simply damaged in the process.

ENDANGERED WILDLIFE

Due to the fast and furious forest exploitation, over 40 species of wildlife, such as the black rhinoceros, gorilla, and elephant, are threatened with extinction. The region is home to several endangered primates, including the Cross River gorilla (*Gorilla gorilla diehli*), a rare endemic subspecies of western gorilla; the mainland drill (*Mandrillus leucophaeus leucophaeus*); and the common chimpanzee (*Pan troglodytes*). In recent years the importance of these animals has been recognized, and parks have been established especially to protect them and their environment. Wildlife in Cameroon includes many exotic species, and the chance to observe these animals closely attracts visitors who love wildlife adventures.

POLLUTION

A young chimpanzee. Chimpanzees are among several primates that make their home in Cameroon.

Urbanization, industrial activities, and a more aggressive exploitation of cultivable land have led to an increase in the amounts of the many pollutants that are discharged and could reach river waters and have a damaging impact on fisheries.

Cameroon has an estimated population of 19,406,100 (2010), living mostly in the towns. Sewerage systems are operating only in newly constructed areas in Yaoundé and Douala. The problem of pollution is under study, and sanitation projects have been started. In Yaoundé some sewerage treatment plants are already effective. Sewerage system projects have also been started in Limbé and Garoua.

PESTICIDES Cacao and coffee plantations use large amounts of pesticides to obtain maximum high-quality yields. These pesticides leach into the nearby waterways, polluting the water and killing fish. Birds may also be affected by ingesting toxic fish. Guidelines are being prepared to establish regulations governing the use of pesticides.

Cameroon Environmental Watch (CEW), a technical partner of World Resource Institute within the Global Forest Watch Program, was founded in 1997 to focus on environmental problems related to critical situations and at-risk areas. One of the issues they have tackled in Cameroon is the hunting and selling of bushmeat without a license, including protected species such as elephants, chimpanzees, and gorillas. By getting the media involved and highlighting environmental issues, there is greater likelihood that these concerns will be managed.

INDUSTRIAL EFFLUENTS Certain industries, such as breweries, food-processing plants, tanneries, and sugar refineries, produce organic waste. Sugar refineries at Nkoteng and Mbandjok discharge sewages straight into the Sanaga River—Cameroon's largest river—without any treatment at all. A tannery and at least three breweries also discharge wastewaters directly into rivers. At Limbé a paper mill and a palm oil factory discharge directly into the sea. These issues are now being addressed because there is a growing awareness of the long-term detrimental effects of pollution on the environment and wildlife, and ultimately on the quality of life in Cameroon. For example, a dam is planned to be built on the Sanaga River that will provide enough water during the dry season to dilute residual discharges from the large pulp mill at Edéa.

FISHERIES

Freshwater fish are very important in Cameroon as they are a common part of the diet. It is particularly urgent, therefore, to protect these fish from pollution. Several mass deaths of villagers in poorly managed river areas have been recorded near Bafussam, caused by oxygen depletion in the water, leading to anoxia (severe lack of oxygen in tissues) in fish. There is a Fisheries Research Station at Limbé that is working to overcome the problems of pollution in the rivers and coastal waters of Cameroon.

CAMEROONIANS

A Cameroonian man with his
motorbike in Houssere Faourou.

> **C**AMEROON HAS A COMPLEX VARIETY of people, which makes it more of a cultural crossroads than most other African states.

In the north many inhabitants live in a Muslim culture that has been influenced by the trans-Saharan Arab world. In the south there is an amalgam of different ethnic groups that itself is rich and diverse even by African standards. The two dominant groups within the Cameroon Highlanders are the Bamiléké and the Tikar.

BAMILÉKÉ AND TIKAR

The majority of people living in the highlands today are Bamiléké, even though their origins lie to the north of Cameroon. They migrated

A modern woman from Douala.

Cameroon is one of Africa's most culturally diverse countries, and with its some 250 ethnic groups and languages, The nation has an extremely varied population. The ethnic groups can be divided into broad linguistic and cultural families corresponding to specific geographic regions of origin and migration.

A Bamiléké in festive costume. The Bamiléké live in the larger towns of Cameroon.

southward around the end of the 16th century. The Bamiléké are thought to be related to the original Bantus, who themselves are thought to have arisen in the western highlands of Cameroon's West Province before spreading across southern Africa. It was the Bantu who first developed the art of working iron and practicing agriculture on an organized scale. Archaeological findings suggest that around 200 B.C. the Bantu began migrating east and south, over time developing into the major ethnic group in Africa south of the Sahara. The prefix *Ba* in the word Bamiléké is itself a Bantu word meaning "the people of."

Traditionally, the Bamiléké society was a highly ordered one that ranked people in social classes from the chief at top, supported by a council of elders, down to slaves. Individual Bamiléké still consider themselves to be members of a specific *fondom* (chiefdom). Of these, the *fondoms* of Bafang, Bafoussam, and Bandjoun are the most prominent. Secret societies were a common feature of Bamiléké social organizations, and they operate today to some extent, although they are not as powerful as they used to be. The most visible characteristic of the Bamiléké people, however, is their domestic architecture—their thatched homes are distinctive evidence of their cultural presence in modern Cameroon.

The Tikar are similar to the Bamiléké in their lifestyle and art forms, but they claim a separate development from an original group of Tikar people about three centuries ago. Smaller groups belonging to the Tikar people are

Tikar women wearing typical village attire.

the Babanki, the Fum, and the Kom. Another of these smaller groups, the Mun, flourished for a short while as an independent kingdom.

THE FULANI

The Fulani people are found in most West African states and also in Central Africa and Sudan. Around A.D. 1000 they migrated southward from northern Africa and began to settle along the coast of West Africa. A Muslim people, the Fulani were involved in various jihads, or holy wars, that led to increases of their power and influence. In the early 19th century a Fulani Empire was established in northern Nigeria and northern Cameroon. This empire was based on an alliance with the Hausa people, following which some intermarriages took place, tightening the knot between the two ethnic groups.

While the Fulani can be found across West Africa, most of them live in northern Cameroon, as do these Fulani children.

Fulani people live and work as pastoralists, grazing their cattle on the savannas. They also farm and grow crops, because this offers some insurance against droughts, which can severely reduce the size and worth of their herds. Their traditional culture attaches a high value to the ownership of cattle: the more animals owned, the higher one's social status in the eyes of the neighbors.

FOREST DWELLERS

In the rain forests of the south live people who have been hunter-gatherers for thousands of years. Baka Pygmies, with an average height of 4.9 feet (1.49 m) are, strictly speaking, pygmoids rather than true pygmies, but in everyday usage the term pygmy is used. These compact people have an intimate relationship with the forest. It provides them with food and shelter, and their whole culture is defined by the forest environment. The pygmies live in small hunting bands.

Baka Pygmies at a dance ceremony. They have a profound relationship with the forest.

MYRIAD GROUPS

Cameroon has so many minority ethnic groups that together they make up a majority of the country's population. Many of them are Bantu-speaking people who over the centuries have migrated toward the coastal areas. They include the Douala, the Bassa, and the Bakoko.

Another Bantu-speaking group is the Bulu. Sometimes referred to as the Boulou, the Bulu are a subdivision of the Fang people who live in Equatorial Guinea and Gabon, as well as Cameroon. The Bulu, who number about half a million in Cameroon, live by hunting and farming and have been influenced by American Protestant missionaries.

In the mountain districts of the northwest, there are various non-Muslim groups that are known collectively as the Kirdi. They include the Bata, the Fali, and the Podoko. The term *Kirdi*, which does not describe any one particular ethnic group, means "people without god" and refers to the fact that they are not Muslims. Thought to have originally come from the east, they gradually retreated farther and farther into the mountains in order to elude more dominant groups such as the Fulani as well as far afield slave-hunting parties.

Kirdi girls. Most Kirdi groups can be found living in the northwestern districts of Cameroon.

Near Lake Chad, the Choa people lead a seminomadic life. Of Arabic origin, they live in large straw houses with grass roofs, each with an enclosed bedroom inside the large house. The area outside the bedroom, sheltered under the big grass roof, serves as a storage area, kitchen, and enclosure for small domesticated animals.

SOCIAL DIFFERENCES

There is a north-south split in Cameroon that tends to create differences between people. As in other African states, the source of the division can be traced back to the historical legacy of colonialism. One important factor in the north-south partition is a religious one: the Muslim-dominated north tends to have a different cultural focus from the Christian-dominated south. There are also economic differences, because the south, where colonialism had more of an impact, is more advanced in terms of education and economic development. The pace of change in the north is slower.

There also exists a social separation between Anglophile and Françophile Cameroonians. What used to be French Cameroon, in the east of the country,

Cameroonian children are more open to interacting with foreigners than are their conservative elders.

had a colonial experience that was different from that in British Cameroon. Many people living in what once was British Cameroon were reluctant to find themselves in a unified state with the Francophile east of the country. This division is still apparent in the choice people make to speak either French or English.

In northern Cameroon the ethnic group that historically has been the most important is the Fulani. Tension between the Fulani and some minority groups has smoldered for many generations. In the south, because the Bamiléké form the majority, ethnic differences are not as distinct.

Cameroon also has nonethnic social divisions that are based on the unequal distribution of wealth in the country. In the larger cities in the south, such as Yaoundé, there are well-educated, sophisticated Cameroonians who lead a lifestyle similar to any other wealthy class of people around the world. The lives of these few people have little in common with the lives of the overwhelming majority of ordinary Cameroonians who are not especially well-to-do.

LIFESTYLE

The dusty streets of Bafoussam.

LIFESTYLES IN CAMEROON REFLECT the mix of cultural groups living in the country. There are features in most people's lives that cut across the cultural divisions, such as a visit to the weekly market.

Because most Cameroonians live and work in the countryside, there are common lifestyle characteristics in this respect as well. In other ways, from house building to the style of one's hair, there are fascinating differences between the cultural groups.

HOMES

In urban centers the structure of buildings is simple. Cinder blocks (they are called breeze blocks in Cameroon) are used to form the walls, and

Typical houses in a Bamenda neighborhood.

Cameroon has an astonishing variety of geographical features and is a country abounding with exceptional social and ethnic diversity. Cameroon's indigenous and modern customs and traditions can be traced back to its diverse ethnic groups and languages, as well as to the influence of European colonialism, Christianity, and Islam.

A view of a village in Cameroon.

sheets of tin make the roofs. A hut rarely stands in isolation, and a village is often simply defined by a compound of homes standing close to one another. The distinction between a small town and a large village is not always clear, but a large village will often have several different compounds, each one consisting of half a dozen huts with walls made of dried mud bricks and separated by bamboo fences.

In small villages and the countryside, a home is more plainly constructed than a house in town. Banana plants, mango trees, and shrubs are planted in gardens surrounding each hut. In addition to providing color and shade, these plants produce food for the family. In a patch of bare scrubland close to the home, a family's goats are tied with rope, and chickens and ducks forage close to their pens.

Villages are often cleaner and neater than an urban compound. In a village each home will have its own latrine. The latrine is actually just a deep hole with a large, flat but lightweight stone as a cover, and for privacy a small screen made with the fiber of leaves from palm trees is used.

A BAMILÉKÉ HOME

The Bamiléké people have had the same basic design for their homes for centuries. The main room is square, and the average length of a wall is about 15 feet (4.6 m). The thatched roof has a distinct conical shape. The walls of the hut are made from mud and bamboo posts. The skill of building is in the construction of a circular platform that rests comfortably and securely on the square walls and supports the conical roof. Creativity and individual expression can be seen in the arrangement of palm fronds around the walls of the hut and in the decorative motifs carved on the bamboo posts or on boards around the entrance.

BUILDING A HOME

The building of a traditional mud hut home, one that does not consist of only cinder blocks and a tin roof, usually starts by placing slender wooden posts into the ground to form the outer walls. A second row of posts is then placed inside the first square to form the inner walls, and the space in between is partially filled with layers of raffia palm laid horizontally at intervals of about a foot and tied to the posts at both ends. This provides a structure for the wall, which is then filled and built up with lumps of mud or dried clay. The corners of the square need more support than can be provided by mud or clay alone, and hard stalks of raffia are inserted to form a sturdy ribbing for the corner joints. Today bricks or cinder blocks are often used for building the corners of rectangular walls.

The grasslands are home to a variety of plants that provide the raw materials for house building. Nails or wire are not needed, and if rope is required to help secure joints, it can be made from the peeled bark of the baobab tree, the fibers of which are pounded together. Mats are made from stalks of millet, which are bunched tightly in clusters and then woven together in a crisscross pattern.

House building is usually reserved for the end of the dry season when there is a lull in agricultural work and plenty of dry grass to use as material.

A villager thatching the roof of his house. Construction of houses is usually carried out during the dry season.

The roof of a house is often built separately and may be finished and put aside until it is needed. Half a dozen people will then help to hoist the prefabricated roof into place. The family will usually celebrate the completion of their new home with a party.

A WOMAN'S LIFE

A Cameroonian woman's life is often more demanding than a man's because she is expected to carry out a long list of daily chores that includes making trips to the local market for food as well as pounding corn or yams to make *fufu* (PHU-phu), a doughy dumpling that is dipped into stews. Fuel for cooking, apart from charcoal, which is purchased, comes in the form of small sticks of wood gathered from the nearest forest. Equally essential is a daily supply of fresh water, and since very few homes enjoy their own tap-water supply, walking to and from the nearest source of water is another

Women are expected to look after all household matters, including fetching water.

daily duty. Women also have the task of looking after their young children and making clothes for them, using cloth purchased in the market and an old sewing machine passed down by the family.

A man's work responsibilities are restricted to clearing land and getting it ready for a new season's planting of cash crops, which he will then tend. The woman may help him with these chores too, and she may devote 6 to 8 hours a day to agriculture in addition to household work. The money that is earned by a man, usually in the wage-labor sector, is typically kept by the man for his own use, but women decide on the use of income from the sale of milk and milk products.

Different ethnic groups have their own traditions defining the role of women and marriage. Such a role is more than establishing a bond between families through marriages. A common practice among many people is that the bridegroom provides the family of the bride with a valuable dowry. This might take the form of an animal, such as an ox. A man can have more than one wife if he can afford a dowry for each of them.

HAIR WITH STYLE

Women in Cameroon, as in many parts of West Africa, distinguish themselves by taking meticulous care of their hairstyle. Large markets will often have hairstylists, each specializing in a particular manner of braiding the hair. Methods and styles of braiding vary from one part of the country to another, and sometimes styling is as popular with men as with women. The braided hair often incorporates an arrangement of beads of varying colors and sizes. These can be threaded into the hair in highly imaginative ways and contribute much to the splendor of many hairdos. Among some Fulani men it is fashionable to have sections of braided hair encased in thin hanging metal strips, preferably bronze, because it can be polished to produce a bright shine.

THE ANLU

Among the Kom people, the Anlu, which means "to drive away," is a women's organization that exists to defend the social and political rights of women. In the late 1950s it became actively involved in a local political demonstration. Within a village community, a Kom woman can call on the Anlu if she feels that there is a need. If a man is responsible for a grievance, such as beating his wife, he can be summoned and asked to apologize or make suitable compensation, depending on the circumstances. There have been cases where a man had repeatedly committed offenses, becoming the target of organized public ridicule by the Anlu to shame him into changing his behavior.

THE LOCAL MARKET

The local market provides people with the daily necessities of life, such as toothpaste, palm oil, rice, cornstarch, and meat. It can be thought of as the African version of a giant supermarket where shoppers can also purchase

Merchants displaying rolls of colorful textiles in a local market.

T-shirts, imported shirts and jeans, plastic shoes, thermos flasks, sugar, printed fabrics for clothing, cigarettes, beer, cotton, and dried foods.

Market day is a big event in a village or small town, especially for the women who have fruit, vegetables, or dairy products to sell, because this is an opportunity to earn a little personal cash. A woman may walk miles to the market to sell just a bag or two of beans she has grown herself. She will set off at dawn from her compound, hoping to secure a prominent place to display her goods. Women also enjoy the opportunity to talk with others. A larger commercial trader will have hired, or will own, a small truck overflowing with a variety of products. The next day he will drive on to another market.

OTHER LIFESTYLES

Northern Cameroon is home to several minorities whose traditional lifestyles are gradually adapting to the mainstream flow of the life of the country.

Mugsum people live in round houses built with mud and stone and covered with roofs made from millet straw.

Kirdi people typically live in compounds like this, perched on a mountainside.

In the far north the Kirdi people have a way of life that differs from people living in the grasslands, the plateaus, or the rain forest. The Kirdi are a pastoral clan who build their farms on the sides of mountains, where a system of terracing has evolved over the centuries to make maximum use of all available land. Terrace walls, which follow the natural contours of the land, are carefully maintained by Kirdi farmers to preserve the physical integrity of each small field.

Close to the border shared with Chad, the Musgum people live around the Logone River, and their dome-shaped homes built of clay and grass are unique. The domes are over 30 feet (9 m) high, and have a small opening at the very top that is closed only during a period of continuous heavy rainfall. The doorways have an unmistakable keyhole shape: narrow at knee-level and then widening out above the hip level.

EDUCATION

In 1999 approximately 81 percent of men aged 15 or over were estimated to be literate, compared with about 69 percent of adult women. This was

Well-dressed children on their way to preschool.

a marked improvement over conditions in 1995 when the figures were approximately 75 percent and 52 percent, respectively. Unfortunately, the latest figures available, from 2001, indicate that males had 77 percent literacy and females only 59.8 percent. There are over 30 teacher-training colleges, 5 institutions of higher education, 6 universities, and a number of other specialized places of higher learning.

When a child reaches the age of around 11, he or she takes the Common Entrance Test—the result of this test largely determines what kind of secondary school the child can attend. There is no age limit for taking the Common Entrance Test. If the results are good, most students and their parents will choose a government school, mainly because government schools do not charge any fees. The second choice for students—mostly those who have unsatisfactory test results—will be a mission school, but these school fees can be too steep for some families. The third choice is usually a private school, but again there are fees to pay, and the academic standards vary greatly from one school to another. Some private remedial schools cater

Students as young as 9 may take the Common Entrance Test, and if they are successful they may begin their secondary education before they turn 10.

to students who fail the Common Entrance Test and wish to improve their standards for another try.

Around the age of 16, pupils take tests run by two examination boards, one based on the British system and the other based on the French system. Students may choose which language to take the examinations in, though the choice is usually determined by the type and location of the secondary school they attend.

In recent years some schools have experienced funding shortfalls. Thus a number of parent and teacher associations have organized their own methods for raising funds and hiring additional teachers.

STAYING IN TOUCH

Cameroon's telephone system is woefully unreliable because of unstable microwave links, as it is based on analog telephone centers that are old and outdated. In 1997 there was less than 1 fixed-line connection per 100 persons. Between 2002 and 2007, partly because of the poor condition and inadequacy of the fixed-line network, mobile phone usage increased more than six times, reaching a subscription base of 25 per 100 persons. This is the first system of its kind in Africa, but whether it is affordable enough for people living in remote rural areas remains to be seen. At the moment only a few public telephones exist outside of towns.

PUBLIC TRANSPORTATION

Private transportation is commonly used for commercial purposes such as transporting goods and delivering supplies. Apart from a small elite in the large cities, few Cameroonians own their own means of transportation. This does not mean they do not travel regularly; quite the contrary, there is an extensive and inexpensive system of public transportation of cars, minibuses, and small trucks. All of them together are popularly called the bush taxi.

Every village and town has its own designated area where bush taxis wait for passengers. There are few scheduled services, other than between the few large cities, and a bush taxi is ready to depart once the seats are filled with passengers and their luggage is secured on the roof rack overhead. Bush taxis travel to the remotest villages—life for most Cameroonians would be unimaginable without them.

HUMAN RIGHTS

Cameroon has a mixed record on human rights. Tension levels rise when election campaigns take place. Despite the democratic infrastructure, the governing party generally shows no intention of relaxing its hold on political power. A human rights case that attracted international attention in the late 1990s concerned Pius Njawé, Cameroon's most famous journalist and editor of the newspaper *Le Messager*. Published three times a week, this paper has a reputation for high editorial standards, but this did not save its editor from official wrath and imprisonment when he published an article about the president.

PROBLEMS

In spite of Cameroon's enviable reputation of economic stability in some aspects, there have also been recent periods of economic hardship. This has resulted in an increase in unemployment, which is causing painful social problems. Although it is regarded as a country with one of the highest school attendance rates in Africa, attendance has dropped-off in some areas. This is partly because parents cannot afford the fees at mission schools and partly because the budgets of government schools have been cut. Not enough school facilities have been added nor have a proportionate number of teachers been hired. Also, the crime rate has increased, and in the far north of the country it is not unusual for travelers to hire armed escorts because of fear of highway robbery. Political and social discord led to civil unrest in 2008, but the shadow of violence has now receded.

About a quarter of rural children are unable to attend school either because their families are poor or because there are insufficient schools in the neighborhood.

RELIGION

Cameroonian Muslims praying during Eid al-Fitr, marking the end of Ramadan, the month of fasting.

A PPROXIMATELY 40 PERCENT OF the Cameroonian population follows traditional African religions, whereas another 40 percent are Christians. Among the Christians, 27 percent are Roman Catholic and 13 percent are Protestant.

The remaining 20 percent of the population adheres to Islam. Freedom of conscience and freedom of religion are guaranteed in the constitution, although the practice of witchcraft is considered a criminal offense.

TRADITIONAL RELIGION

Traditional religion is a general name for the great variety of indigenous beliefs of African societies. These are not religions in the institutional sense of Christianity and Islam, and there is no set of dogma nor a holy text, such as the Bible or the Koran. There is, however, the unifying belief that nature is invested with spiritual forces and that there is a need to coexist peacefully with these unseen powers. There is a shared sense of continuity between the living and the dead, especially the recently dead, and a belief that communication between the two worlds is sometimes possible. That explains why in some parts

Right: The king's *achum*, or spirit house, in Bafut.

The pervasive respect for life and the people's affinity with the dead inspired the national anthem of Cameroon.

O Cameroon, thou cradle of our fathers,
Holy shrine where in our midst they now repose,
Their tears and blood and sweat thy soil did water,
On thy hills and valleys once their tillage rose.
Dear fatherland, thy worth no tongue can tell.
How can we ever pay thy due?
Thy welfare we will win in toil and love and peace,
Will be to thy name ever true!

Chorus:
Land of promise, land of glory!
Thou, of life and joy, our only store.
Thine be honor, thine devotion,
And deep endearment, for evermore.

To ordinary residents of a community, a diviner is an intermediary between the physical and the spiritual worlds.

of Cameroon the deceased are buried inside the family home. Some Kirdi groups have soul jars stored in the vicinity of their homes so that the dead spirits will have their own homes. A soul jar is similar to a small family shrine, and remembrance offerings are made on special occasions. The shrine of an ancestor will often contain an item once owned by the ancestor.

Ancestor worship is an important aspect of traditional religion. Recently deceased kin are seen as living beings who continue to watch over their family and their village. Thus people take care not to do anything that might offend these powerful living dead.

DIVINERS

Diviners are recognized and accepted by the community as possessing special skills that allow them to discover, or divine, supernatural aspects of life. The attributes that diviners possess are a combination of intuitive knowledge and acquired skills built up over a lifetime of living and working in the community. The sense of the diviner as someone possessing magical and supernatural powers is reinforced by the way in which divination is achieved through special means—although the means often are changed every day. In western Cameroon, for example, spider divination is practiced using earth spiders, or sometimes the land crab, both of which live in underground burrows. A spider diviner will have a small shrine of his own around the entrance to one of these burrows. When a villager seeks advice, the diviner will place special cards, inscribed with symbolic markings, inside the burrow. The cards, known as leaf cards because they are made from the leaves of a plum tree, are arranged around some tasty, freshly captured insects or some highly edible fresh green leaves that are used as bait. In the process of eating the bait, the spider tampers the arrangement of the leaf cards, and it is the new configuration of the cards that the diviner interprets for its message.

Fine carving on the wall of an ancient shrine.

Another traditional means of obtaining a reading is to use a crab shell that is filled with wet sand inscribed with symbols and pierced with small sticks. This mixture is poured over a river crab, and after a period of time while the crab moves around, the diviner interprets the new pattern of the mixture. The new arrangement of sticks and the scrambling of the symbols is interpreted as a communication from a spirit.

Women attending a church service.

CHRISTIANITY

Most Cameroonian Christians are Roman Catholic. Diverse groups making up the Protestant faith are Presbyterian, Baptist, and Lutheran. The distribution of Christians and Muslims follows a geographical split, with more Muslims in the north, while most Christians are found in the south of the country.

A church service in a Christian church is likely to be filled with music and songs that rely on traditional African rhythms. This willingness of Christian churches to adapt their practices to harmonize with indigenous religions accounts for the successful spread of Christianity across Cameroon and Africa in the 20th century.

MISSIONARIES

Christianity was first introduced to Cameroon in the first half of the 19th century. One of the earliest recorded interventions was the arrival of the

Dressed in their Sunday best, children at play in the churchyard.

Baptist Missionary Society of London in 1844. In 1858 land was purchased from the Bimbia chiefs, and the first religious settlement, a Baptist church, was built there. Baptist missionaries led by the Reverend Alfred Saker founded the town of Victoria, since 1982 called Limbé. Under German colonial rule, Catholic and Presbyterian groups arrived from Germany and the United States, and bitter conflicts were ignited between the different missions as they jockeyed for influence. They were not allowed, however, to operate at all in Muslim areas.

Missionaries were initially very intolerant of the beliefs and practices of indigenous African religions. Newly converted Africans were forbidden to dance to their traditional village music because it was associated with pagan celebrations. People being indoctrinated with Christianity came to feel ashamed of their own cultures and were induced to leave them behind. The attitude of missionaries has changed a lot since then, and their stark intolerance has been replaced by acceptance of many aspects of the traditional belief system.

BLACK CHURCHES

Until the 1960s the majority of churches remained securely under the control of whites. As congregations grew, so did the need to recruit and train local people as instructors and clergy. The advent of an African dimension to Christianity was warmly welcomed. Today this is revealed in the tremendous popularity and spread of independent churches that have adapted their chosen Christian religion to go well with African traditions. The roles of ancestor worship, polygamy, and traditional medicine were areas of belief that earlier missionaries did not accept, but the new independent churches are more willing to try to integrate these beliefs into their own dogmas. Traditional medicine, for instance, overlaps with the notion of faith healing that is fairly common in some evangelical churches. Moreover, some churches accept, or turn a blind eye to, the practice of polygamy.

ISLAM

Islam originated among the Arab people in Saudi Arabia in the seventh century A.D. and rapidly spread north and west, reaching Tunisia by A.D. 670

Muslim boys studying the Koran, which calls for close repetition.

hajj:	*the pilgrimage to Mecca, one of the five pillars of Islamic faith.*
imam:	*a Muslim prayer leader.*
muezzin:	*the person who calls Muslims to prayer by chanting loudly from a mosque's minaret.*
Koran:	*the religious text (book) or law of Islam, containing the sacred words of Allah as revealed to the Prophet Muhammad.*
salat (SAL-at):	*the daily prayer ritual, carried out five times a day.*
sawm (sow-UM):	*fasting, especially during the month of Ramadan.*

and advancing across North Africa and into Spain and Portugal. Most of North Africa fell to Muslim rule, and trans-Saharan trade carried the new religion to West Africa, as Arab merchants traveled across the caravan routes of the desert to trade salt for gold from West Africa. What is now northern Nigeria developed important trading centers, and in this way Islam found its way to Cameroon.

Islam, which means "submission to God," believes in one god, Allah, and his prophet, Muhammad, who was born in Mecca in Saudi Arabia around A.D. 570. Muhammad received his first revelations from God around 610. Muslims also believe in angels who deliver the word of God to ordinary people, and in the 28 prophets who received instruction from God. Jesus Christ was one of these prophets, along with Abraham, David, and Moses.

Muslims are bound to adhere to the five pillars of Islam. These are professing one's faith to Allah, praying five regular times a day, fasting during the holy month of Ramadan, donating a share of one's wealth to the poor, and making a pilgrimage to Mecca at least once during one's lifetime.

Ramadan is the most important month of the Muslim year. Its date changes from one year to the next because it is determined by the lunar calendar. During the month of Ramadan, Muslims have to fast (*saum*), which means they are not allowed to eat or drink between sunrise and sunset. A joyous three-day festival, Eid al-Fitr, celebrates the end of Ramadan.

LANGUAGE

A girl in class. Frananglais, a mix of French, English, and Creole, is discouraged in schools.

FRENCH AND ENGLISH are Cameroon's official languages, but the country has a bewildering linguistic diversity of 24 major African language groups, from at least 250 different ethnic groups.

People living within a few miles of each other may speak different dialects of the same language, which explains why places and people often have more than one name. The Fulani, for example, are also known as the Fula, the Fulanke, the Fulbe, the Fellata, and the Peulh.

FRANANGLAIS

With nearly 280 indigenous languages, plus French and English as official languages, it can be tricky to choose the right vocabulary

Radio broadcasting reaches the far corners of the nation. Women are increasingly becoming more involved in nontraditional roles.

to convey a message. Cameroonian youths spontaneously deviate from linguistic rules with the objective of being able to communicate easily, and the resulting lingo has become known as Frananglais. It is a mixture of French, English, and Creole. "*Je veux go*" is a mixture of French and English and means "I want to go" or "I'm leaving." Or a child might say "*Tout le monde hate me, wey I no know,*" which means "Everybody hates me, I don't know why." Frananglais is not an official language, and its use has been discouraged in schools across the country because teachers say it has a corrosive influence on correctly spoken and written English and French.

FRENCH AND ENGLISH

French is the more commonly used of the two official languages. English is seldom heard except in the large cities. This is because French Cameroon was a far larger state than British Cameroon. Pidgin English, a simplified version

A sign indicating the direction to Central Station in both English and French.

A signboard announcing services in both English and French.

of spoken English, is used mainly in Anglophile areas and less commonly in Francophile regions. Standard English is rarely used, for it is reserved for formal occasions and tends to be spoken only by the highly educated. When Cameroonians find that they do not share a common local language, English or French is used as a practical way of communicating. A native speaker of English or French would find it difficult to understand what is being said, and their speech would not be easily understood by the locals in many everyday situations. Most of the African languages spoken in Cameroon are tonal languages, which means the tone of the voice actually changes the meaning of a word. This linguistic characteristic spills over to the pronunciation of English and is heard in pidgin English.

PIDGIN ENGLISH

There are several varieties of pidgin English, an informal way of communicating in English. It has developed, with regional variations, in nearly all countries where English is spoken but is not a native tongue. It started in east Asia and is now used in the Caribbean, West Africa, and some Pacific Islands. Pidgin English has been spoken in Cameroon for about 300 years, and it is sometimes mistakenly thought of as a very simplified form of English. This may help explain its origins, but it does not do justice to the complexity of pidgin English, which can be regarded as a language in its own right, with its own grammar and vocabulary. Common verbs, such as *have* or *did*, are frequently omitted, and the letter *s* is often left off the end of a word. "No tok dat bad people" contains the pidgin word *tok* for "talk" and *dat* for "that"; the sentence expresses a warning about talking to someone pointed out as being undesirable company.

A young man, for example, may start a conversation with a woman by asking her where she is going, "E! Ma sista, usai you di go?" He may suggest a visit to the local town, "Make we shake skin for ville." The word *ville* comes from French, whereas *shake skin* is pidgin for "to get going" or "to move."

If someone is asking a companion whether he had a good night's sleep, he may ask, "You sleep fine?" or "Day don clean?" The word *don*, a familiar pidgin expression derived from "done," is often used in a variety of situations

Pidgin English, spoken by many Cameroonians, is not easily understood or picked up by foreigners.

"My friend is my friend." Women companions enjoying a party.

to express the idea of something completed. For example the sentence, "I don chop fine" means "I've eaten well." A fine chop means "a hearty meal."

Even within pidgin English there are variations in sentence structure (syntax), grammar, and vocabulary. Some linguists use the term "educated pidgin" to describe one type of pidgin English. For example someone may say, "My friend is my friend," which means that the person is a close and trusted friend.

Linguists have compiled pidgin English dictionaries, but the origin of many words and even whole expressions is not always known or understood. For instance, it is common to refer to a good friend as "my *combe*" (kom BAY), but it is unknown whether the word *combe* is derived from the English word *comrade* or whether it originates from a local language. What is known is that pidgin English is a highly developed and creative language that cannot be picked up by a native English speaker in a couple of days. Proficient speakers of pidgin English, when traveling across the country, often find new words and expressions that have evolved solely in one area. Furthermore, due to a constant process of mixing and borrowing, similar to any living language, pidgin English is always changing.

MASTERS OF LANGUAGE

In Cameroon, because there is no single language used by everyone, switching from one language to another is common. Linguists call this practice "code-switching." In the course of one day, Cameroonians may need to use up to six different languages. For example, they may speak in English in the former British Cameroon, switch to French when talking to someone from French Cameroon, and converse with market vendors and their family members using the local dialects.

BANTU SPEAKERS

The first Bantu speakers in Africa lived in northern Cameroon for hundreds of years and then, sometime around the first century A.D., began to move south. This migration was to have momentous consequences in terms of language. The relocation took place gradually over centuries, and as Bantu groups split off from the main population movement and settled down elsewhere, various Bantu dialects developed. By the year 1500 most of the central, eastern, and southern parts of Africa were inhabited by Bantu speakers. Their descendants

Cameroon is so linguistically diverse that it is not uncommon to find a village or small town having two or even three different names.

A Bantu-speaking cattle owner. Many minority languages in Cameroon are Bantu-based.

A speaker greeting a friend will often say "mia yu" (ME-ah-u), but if they are talking to strangers, they may say "mia ka" (ME-ah-car). In another local language, Nwe, a person will say "hello" by uttering "alele" (AL-lay-e) and "good-bye" by wishing the person "go gan bon" (go-GAN-bon); the latter expression means "you travel well." Although the French word bon *means "good," linguists have argued that this is just a coincidence and that the word is not derived from French.*

Saying hello to someone is sometimes not a simple matter of uttering one or two words. Like all languages, African ones can be finely tuned to suit the occasion. When two people meet, the relationship and situation may require more than the word "hello." Sometimes, even if the intention is merely to briefly greet one another then say farewell, an outside observer might guess they are having a long and meaningful conversation. It would be seen as rude to simply exchange only a few words and then go their separate ways.

later migrated south from the Adamawa Plateau toward the coast. About 300 Bantu languages and dialects are now spoken across Africa.

FULFULDE AND BALI

The language of the Fulani is Fulfulde, a member of the Niger-Congo group of West African languages. Fulfulde is strikingly different from English. The plural of a Fulfulde word is formed by changing the first consonant and the word ending, whereas in English a change to the end of a word is usually sufficient to indicate a plural. In Fulfulde a plural often looks and sounds like a completely different word.

Bali, another local tongue in Cameroon, was one of the first languages adopted by missionaries in their endeavors to communicate with and convert indigenous people. German missionaries, and later the English, promoted Bali as a lingua franca, a common language used among speakers of different languages. The clerics also translated the Bible into Bali.

ARTS

A craftsman pouring bronze into a mold for a small sculpture.

>C AMEROON IS RICH IN ARTS AND crafts largely because of the variety of cultural groups that make up the country. The grasslands region, comprised of numerous small Bantu-speaking societies, is particularly noted for its wooden masks. In the same area the Kirdi people are very well known for their pottery and the Tikar are famous for their elaborately decorated brass pipes.

Traditional art is an expression of indigenous religious rites and mysteries. When exhibited in museums overseas, many Cameroonian

Art plays an important role in Cameroonian daily life. Most art forms in Cameroon are based on ethnic traditions. Some crafts, such as wood carving, basket weaving, cloth embroidering, batik work, and calabash decorating, showcase the variety of art in daily life.

A village elder preparing for a ritual. Only the most intricately woven cloth can be used during rituals.

A face carving on the door post of a chief's palace.

works are not seen within the context they were created for, and therefore these items are not fully appreciated. Carved human figures were usually produced for a special purpose. For example, some were kept near the entrance of a home to guard the place while the family was out working, and small figurines of pregnant women were handheld during fertility dances.

GRASSLANDS ART

The grasslands of western Cameroon are home to the Bamiléké and Tikar peoples. Their art includes carved masks and figures made from wood and ivory. Popular subjects are human heads, often shown with wide, gaping mouths, and animals such as elephants, crocodiles, snakes, panthers, and tortoises. The spider, an important participant in divination, is one of the most commonly seen motifs. Detailed figures are carved into lavishly decorated house posts of traditional homes, standing on either side of the entrance. Common domestic items, such as beds and bedposts, bowls, and drinking horns, are also carved with great skill. Chiefs possess intricately carved thrones and stools.

In traditional Bamiléké culture, only the chief and a few other high-ranking individuals are permitted to wear an elephant mask during ceremonies or festivities. The elephant, acclaimed as one of the mighty animals of the land, is a symbol of the status and wealth of local chiefs and kings. In some clan legends the chief has the magical power to turn himself into an elephant. Worn with the mask is an elaborate costume, decorated to draw attention to the high rank of the wearer, and glass beads, which date back to the days of the slave trade when they were used as a form of currency.

Teen boys masquerading at a festival.

THE BEAUTY OF BEADS

A distinctive art form in Cameroon is the use of beads to decorate wooden sculptures. In past centuries beads were valuable because they were not easily available and came only by way of trade with Nigeria. Beads, such as pierced cowrie shells, also became a form of currency, and possession of them signified high social status. For this reason, the wearing of exquisite bead jewelry and the use of objects decorated with beads were restricted to royal families. Examples of beaded throne stools include a sacred seat used for royal occasions that has been preserved from the precolonial era. Other beaded items include calabashes (gourds), bottles, and pipe stems. No longer limited to royals, present-day Cameroonian women like to wear bead necklaces.

In the 20th century the art of bead embroidery was developed by self-employed artisans hoping to sell their work to tourists and other travelers. While the original craftspeople were employed only by royalty, it is now common for such work to be carried out by groups of village women working in cooperatives. The range of objects that are embroidered with beads is basically the same as it was in the past: bowls, calabash containers, and stools, as well as figures of lizards and birds, but clothing and jewelry such as bracelets and even beaded shoes are also seen nowadays.

The raw materials—cloth, thread, and beads—are purchased by a cooperative from a local market, whereas the wooden sculpture or the calabash that serves as a base is commissioned directly from a local wood-carver. The first stage involves cutting the cloth to match exactly the sculptured shape and then attaching the cloth to the shape. The threaded beads are then sewn onto the cloth. The artisan makes sure that there is no space between the individual beads or the rows of beads. The designs are produced from memory or improvised while working. It takes two days to embroider a small object, one week to finish a bird, and three months or more to complete a large calabash. The work is time-consuming because it is all done without the use of any machine. Moreover, extreme care must be taken to integrate the decorative motif, a spider or a lizard, for example, into the pattern. Women in their cooperatives usually work on bead embroidery after the harvest when they have time to spare.

A woman wearing beads, popular adornments from precolonial times.

POTTERY

Pottery serves many functions in Cameroon. Special pots are made for ritual occasions, celebrating different stages of the life cycle. For example, the birth of twins merits a unique Siamese-style pot with two openings at the top.

Some of the most valuable Cameroonian art is pottery crafted solely for the benefit of the local chiefs. These pots are decorated with traditional motifs of animal figures, often represented in whimsical poses such as playfully

The Kim, one of the small groups making up the Bamiléké people, have an artistic tradition of carving life-size portraits of their chiefs. The Afo-a-Kom is one of a series of three such beaded sculptures of the Fun Yoho fons, a very powerful family credited with semidivine attributes. Afo-a-Kom means "Kom's thing," and to Kom people it is a symbol of dynasty. In 1966 the Afo-a-Kom was stolen from the Kom capital of Laikom and became international news when it later turned up for sale in New York. Seven years after the theft, it was finally returned to Laikom. The theft focused world attention on the phenomenon of international art theft in Africa. An unexpected consequence of this crime was to encourage Cameroonians, and the Kom in particular, to treasure their own artistic heritage. Before its disappearance, the Afo-a-Kom had not been seen by many Cameroonians, but world media abruptly brought it to their attention. The theft also reignited the interest of Western art collectors in African art. Afoakom-USA was founded in 2003 as a nonprofit organization committed to protecting the cultural heritage of the Kingdom of Kom, including the preservation of Kom culture among Kom people living in the United States.

dancing lizards. Areas where such pottery was traditionally made are today producing high-quality pottery for export to Europe and the United States.

Beautiful pots are also made for ordinary household use. These clay pots are sold throughout the country. In western Cameroon there is a tradition of making *mimbo* (MEEM-boh) pots, which have extra large rims to prevent the water or wine inside from spilling. The exteriors of these pots are decorated with sculptures of animals.

ROYAL ARCHITECTURE

Bamiléké culture is distinguished by its traditionally styled village huts. Some of the royal huts, built in the past for their chiefs, survive to this day. One of the best-preserved examples of royal architecture is the impressive Bandjoun Palace, located near the town of Bafoussam. It is a large circular compound,

Intricately detailed totemic carvings adorn the facade of Bandjoun Palace.

over 50 feet (15 m) in circumference, with a second circle of 20-foot (6-m) tall carved wooden poles built up outside the compound. These poles support the single thatched roof of the reception hall that would have been used as a court and for assemblies. There are huts for the chief and separate huts for each of the chief's wives, all with elaborately decorated doorways. The paths in the palace complex all lead to the village square, which serves as a public area for personal appearances by the *fon* and as the weekly marketplace.

MUSIC AND DANCE

Cameroon has an exuberant cultural tradition in music and dance. Many of the different ethnic groups have developed their own distinctive styles of dancing and accompanying music that are an integral part of Cameroonian festivals, ceremonies, social gatherings, and storytelling. Traditional dances are elegantly choreographed, though the musical accompaniment may be as simple as stamping feet and clapping hands. Traditional

Royal compounds such as the Bandjoun Palace have been called the last cathedrals of the Bamiléké tradition.

Xylophones are popular instruments in Cameroon and are featured in many bands.

instruments include bells worn by dancers, clappers, whistles, drums, talking drums, flutes, rattles, scrapers, horns, stringed instruments, and xylophones. The combination varies with each ethnic group and region—and event. In the south the xylophone and the drum are featured in nearly every band. In the north Hausa music from Nigeria, characterized by a highly percussive sound and loud drum music, is popular. Francis Bebey (1929—2001)—a famous Cameroonian musician and singer—successfully blended traditional dance rhythms and instruments with more modern sounds. In 2008 the famous Australian classical guitarist John Williams recorded a track entitled "Hello Francis," an homage to his dear friend, using one of Bebey's favorite rhythms, the *makossa*.

Cameroon's musical heritage is at its richest in the south because the port towns there play host to a grand variety of influences from African and Western countries. A result of this fusion was *asiko* (A-see-ko) music, which brought together traditional instruments, such as the xylophone, with a Western instrument, such as the acoustic guitar. What really swept the country, though, was *makossa* music, and its enormous popularity lasted through all of the 1970s and 1980s. Although much of the impetus behind Cameroonian music comes from male bands, female musicians have also made their mark. In the early 1980s Bebe Manga became one of the most successful singers in Africa, and her enchanting songs were hits in French-influenced parts of the West Indies.

Successful Cameroonian musicians include Sam Fan Thomas and Moni Bilé. Sam Fan Thomas is one of the country's best-known guitarists and is an important figure in the development of zouk music. Born in 1952 in western Cameroon, Thomas's albums include *Funky New Bell* and *Rikiatou*. Moni Bilé, born in 1957 in Douala, is also a guitarist. His band music weds popular Cameroonian percussive sounds with rich drumbeats from the Democratic Republic of the Congo (formerly Zaire). His success as a musician arises from his ability to develop the enormously popular *makossa* dance rhythms. This style of music was successfully pioneered in the early 1970s by Manu Dibango, a famous musician in Cameroon.

Manu Dibango has made an enormous contribution to African music as a whole. His nickname is The Lion of Cameroon, from a track on *The Very Best of African Soul* album. In 2007 Dibango celebrated 50 years in music with the release of a CD/DVD *The Lion of Africa*.

The Dance of the Princesses, performed with complex xylophone accompaniment.

ZOUK MUSIC

Zouk music is a blend of African and Caribbean music that developed in the 1980s. It has now become one of the most popular musical forms in Cameroon. Zouk music is also well liked in other parts of western and central Africa. This captivating new genre of music originated in Paris when West Indian bands started performing with and influencing musicians from Cameroon and the Democratic Republic of the Congo (Zaire).

Zouk music first became known outside of Africa and the West Indies when its hi-tech electronic rhythms, which combine African drums with Caribbean percussion, began to dominate the discos of Paris. In terms of musical culture, zouk has a fascinating trajectory because it can be traced back to Africa for its structural rhythms and harmony and then across the Atlantic to the Caribbean, where it was enriched by mellowed European traditions, long ago imported by the colonial powers. Now it has returned to West Africa via the musical melting pot of Paris. Important zouk musicians in Cameroon are Toto Guillaume and Jules Kamga.

TOBACCO PIPES

Tobacco was introduced to Africa in the 16th century, and pipe smoking became popular with men and women. The design of a pipe depended on the social status of the smoker, and many of the exquisite examples of carved pipes from Cameroon that are seen in museums around the world were made for chiefs. Their elaborately carved pipes served a ritual purpose and were smoked during fertility festivals. Carved from a variety of materials—clay, metal, gourds, and stone—some of the pipes had skillfully crafted designs decorating the stem and the pot, which holds tobacco or hemp.

Western Cameroon was noted for its clay pipe-making skills, and many of the finest examples of pipes were made there. Only men manufactured them, and there were rules about what patterns could be inscribed on the pipes. An ordinary person could not afford to have more than a geometric pattern carved on his or her pipe, but a wealthier patron might commission

Manu Dibango, born December 12, 1933, is Cameroon's most famous and influential musician. He is now an international star and the best-known Cameroonian musician outside his own country. In 1983, at the age of 50, his receptiveness to new musical styles remained undiminished when he recorded a single called "Abele Dance," which fused African rhythms with those of New York's hip-hop sounds. He went on to produce his own album, Electric Africa, *which continued to explore ways of joining contemporary electronic music with traditional African rhythms.*

Dibango, born in the coastal town of Douala, first went to France in 1949 to further his studies. He became a saxophonist and pianist and was influenced by the African music coming from the Democratic Republic of the Congo (Zaire). In 1963 he returned to Cameroon. After a couple of years, he was back in Europe. When he returned to Douala in 1971, he took the country by storm with his hit "Soul Makossa." This song also became a big hit in the United States and turned Dibango into an international star.

Manu Dibango has pushed forward the frontiers of African music by opening up its traditional rhythms to modernist musical trends from Europe and North America. In his own words, he wants "to let people know that there is an electric Africa also; that people there are dealing with electricity and with computers. Our music isn't going to be only in museums any more. Because Africa is in the Third World, maybe people are thinking that African musicians aren't able to play pianos, synths, or saxes. They want to see Africans beating tom-toms and talking drums. But things are changing."

an animal to be carved. Only the chief has the honor of owning a pipe carved with human and animal figures.

NOVELISTS

Most Cameroonian novelists write in French, although their work is often translated into English. Mongo Beti, one of the foremost writers of Africa's independence generation, was born as Alexandre Biyidi (or Biyidi-Awala) in 1932. In his early works, such as *Poor Christ of Bomba* and *King Lazarus,*

Beti exposes the injustices of colonialism and the racist attitudes it fosters. Novelists and other artists are dissuaded from any examination of contemporary political ills, and censorship largely ensures that such issues do not appear in print. Beti gets around this problem in his later novels by not setting the stories in Cameroon but creating characters and situations that reflect Cameroonian society.

Ferdinand Oyono (1929—2010), is one of the most renowned anticolonialist novelists of Africa. In Cameroon as a child he was a choirboy in the Catholic church, and he studied with a priest. After earning his diploma, he worked as a servant for missionaries and then studied at a high school in France before finishing his education at French universities, writing his first novels at that time. He wrote three novels in his twenties: *Un vie de boy* (1956), *Le Vieux Nègre et la médaille* (1956), and *Chemin d'Europe* (1960). These novels continue to merit wide readership and favorable critical interest. His novels are representative of the period in which he wrote since they focus on the injustices of the colonial system.

An actor performing as the king of a tribe.

Mongo Beti's novel *Perpetua and the Habit of Unhappiness* is recognized as an indictment of the way his country was governed under President Ahmadou Ahidjo. This work is banned in Cameroon.

DRAMA

Conflicts between traditional and modern aspects of cultural life are familiar themes in Cameroonian drama. When young people leave their village community and experience urban life, they are introduced to behaviors and attitudes that often clash with those they were brought up with. This becomes a source of deep family pain and conflict when parents, who adhere to traditional beliefs and customs, cannot understand the way their children have changed. One common theme in dramas is a family's arguing about the choice of a husband or wife. This dilemma is examined in Léon-Marie Ayissi's play *Les Innocents* (*The Innocents*), which deals with problems that arise when a young man seeks to choose his own marriage partner.

LEISURE

Young girls singing and dancing behind a boy standing at a marimba.

MUSIC, DANCE, AND ENJOYING THE company of friends and family are defining features in Cameroonian leisure. Sociability, as much an African characteristic as it is Cameroonian, lies at the heart of countless festivals and in the way people spend their leisure time.

The country is not immune to electronic forms of entertainment: in the cities digital video games are popular. Such imported kinds of entertainment, however, have not overturned the appeal of traditional African games such as mancala, a family of board games.

A girl playing with a balloon.

Each of Cameroon's ethnic groups has its own unique folkways. Throughout the year seven national holidays are observed. Cameroonians totally enjoy these social occasions. Festivals with music and dance are integral parts of these gatherings. Soccer is very popular and many boys dream of playing on the national team.

The Cameroonian National Soccer Team is a source of great pride for the country.

SOCCER

Soccer is very popular in Cameroon, and interest in the sport is growing due to the successes of the national team. Cameroon has qualified for the FIFA World Cup six times—in 1982, 1990, 1994, 1998, 2002, and 2010—more than any other African nation. The team, called The Indomitable Lions, qualified for the quarter finals in the 1990 World Cup, losing to England in extra time. In 1984, 1988, 2000, and 2002 they won the Africa Cup of Nations and in 2000 they took home the gold medal at the Summer Olympics held in Sydney, Australia. Soccer fans in 2010 especially cheered their hero, Samuel Eto'o, who was proclaimed African player of the year three times.

A RACE UP MOUNT CAMEROON

An annual event in February that attracts many international sportsmen is known as The Mount Cameroon Race of Hope. This marathon involves a race

Elephants, as well as leopards, are respected as creatures that control their environment. For this reason they may represent a king or an object with political influence in a fable.

from the Molyko Sports Complex in Buea to the top of Mount Cameroon, an active volcano. The course spans a total distance of 26 miles (41.8 km). In 2009 the cash prize was $10,000. The starting lineup in 2010 was over 700 runners. More than 50,000 spectators watch the athletes complete the race in less than four hours.

THINKING WITH ANIMALS

A fable is a story with a moral lesson. Most African fables revolve around animals. The telling of fables has been part of African culture for untold centuries, and it continues to this day. Adults and children love to gather in a common village compound to listen to a fable, and storytelling is a shared leisure experience that the entire community enjoys.

The pleasure that people gain from these fables and their function within African societies can be best understood when the significance of certain

A FULANI FABLE ABOUT REWARDS *In the middle of the night, when mostly everyone was asleep, a man looking at the sky through his telescope spotted a cow hanging from the moon by a long rope. The cow looked healthy and was mooing loudly, so the man called his friend who was a hunter. Carefully aiming his arrow at the hanging rope, the hunter cut through it. The cow fell to earth and landed in a river. Before the hunter could get to the cow, a fisherman caught it by the horns with his fishing line and dragged it to shore, but the cow quickly ran off, attracted by the sound of mooing from a nearby field. The cow joined other cows in the field, and that evening, the farmer who owned the field stood admiring the new addition to his herd, thinking how lucky he was. This story suggests that those who do the work don't always get the reward!*

A DOUALA FABLE ABOUT TWO CATS *A man was becoming increasingly worried because his chickens had been disappearing mysteriously from his henhouse every night. He suspected the thief was his own cat, but the cat protested her innocence. The man decided to set a trap. He used one of his chickens as bait and built a clever trapdoor that would snap closed and confine the thief. The next morning, much to his surprise, he found a bush cat—an African wildcat—inside the trap. From then on, no more of his chickens disappeared. So be careful about accusing someone unless you have some evidence.*

A DOUALA FABLE ABOUT STRENGTH *The wind liked to blow hard and show off to everyone, "I'm so powerful, I can blow all day and all night and at anyone I like. No one is stronger than I." But a small swallow took up his challenge and told him, "Blow as hard as you wish. Birds can still fly." The wind laughed aloud and challenged all the birds to try to resist his power. The hawk was the first to try, but the wind turned into a mighty storm. In the end the struggling hawk gave up. Next, the eagle tried. Although it could fly very fast, it could not keep up against the wind. Eventually it gave up. The third bird was a heron. It managed to resist the strong wind for only a very short time and quickly broke a wing trying. The last bird to take up the wind's challenge was the swallow. Being small, it could dive and dart around and successfully resist the wind. This tale teaches you that strength and skill is not a matter of size and that boasting gets you nowhere.*

animals is taken into account. A French anthropologist, Claude Lévi-Strauss, wrote that particular animals are used because they represent important values. Lions, for example, mean courage. Some of the animals used in tales may have become extinct, but that does not lessen their significance in a story because the animals are seen as humans in disguise.

MANCALA

Mancala is a family of board games, and *warri* (WAR-ree) is the Cameroonian version of the game. It is played across Africa, especially in West Africa, using a board with two rows of six scooped-out holes or cups. Also called *awele* (a-wee-LEE), the objective of the game is to capture the playing pieces or markers, which are seeds, pebbles, or anything else suitable in size, that rest in your opponent's holes in the board. At either end of the board there is a small cup that collects the captured markers for each player. Although the rules are simple, the subtleties of playing are what makes the game so fascinating.

Women gathered for a board game after a day of work.

Mancala is regarded as one of the earliest two-player strategy games in the world. Despite widespread popularity across most parts of Africa and Asia, it remains fairly unknown in Europe and North America.

VILLAGE BARS

Villages usually have a bar serving beer and nonalcoholic juices. The bar functions as an acceptable place for men and women to meet. Millet, sorghum, and corn can be fermented to make local beer, but today trucks deliver bottled beer to the most remote corners of the country. In coastal areas people enjoy palm wine as well.

MUSIC

Playing musical instruments, listening to music, and dancing are essential elements in Cameroonian leisure activities. People do not simply purchase recordings of their favorite singers or groups and listen to them in the privacy of their homes, as in the West. Playing music and dancing together in West Africa is a form of popular public culture, one that people participate in as a group. There is a healthy urban musical tradition in Cameroon, but outside of the cities, there are very few professional musicians. Nearly every community has the resources to produce music to brighten up a social gathering or a

Drums are featured in most Cameroonian celebrations, providing the life beat of the occasions.

special event. The xylophone is one of the most popular instruments and can be easily made using a frame of bamboo placed over dried gourds that act as resonators for the sounds. Drums are not expensive to make and turn up in most village events where music is called for. There are also some specialized instruments that are not commonly found elsewhere. Women play the *oding* (oh-DING), a flutelike instrument that produces light airy music.

DANCING

Social events everywhere are enlivened by dancing, and urban Cameroon has its own fast-paced dance style called *makossa*. This dance dates back to the 1970s when mission schools used school bands as part of school life; for instance, music accompanied the stream of students in and out of daily assemblies.

During the planting season, a group of women—as many as 20 or more—will often gather for a drink after a hard day's work in the fields. The village square is a common meeting place for such informal parties, when local beer is passed around in large gourds. Often there is impromptu dancing and singing, with clapping from passersby gathered in a circle around the performers.

Women dancing casually in the street. Dancing is a big part of the social lives of Cameroonians.

FESTIVALS

Bamiléké dancers at a celebration.

CHAPTER 12

N CAMEROON IT IS UNCOMMON to find the kind of national public festivals such as Christmas and Thanksgiving that have become institutionalized in Europe and North America. Instead, there is an astonishing diversity of local festivals for an equally diverse sea of occasions.

Major stages in the life cycle, such as birth, puberty, marriage, and death, are celebrated, as also are important agricultural events. Yam festivals, for example, take place in parts of southern Cameroon when the important food staple roots are ready for harvesting.

Women wearing brightly painted helmets made of calabash in celebration of the annual millet beer festival in Tourou village.

Annual traditional festivals provide occasions for colorful dances and carnivals. Some festivals have a deep spiritual significance, while others offer traditional dances and choral music, handicraft exhibitions, pageantry, parades, parties, and competitive sports. In short, fun for all.

117

Muslims gathered to commemorate the end of Ramadan, the holy month of fasting.

FESTIVE OCCASIONS

The death of a clan chief and the initiation of a new one may be only a local event, but it will be observed in a major way. In western Cameroon there is a traditional April festival where the tribal chief disappears into a cave, only to reappear later, as if reborn in the spring, when a ritual procession makes its way to the mouth of the cave. The village diviner marks the foreheads of participants with a mixture of camwood and water, and women are blessed for their continued fertility.

Another joyous celebration is the completion of the harvest around the month of February. Ritualistic harvest festivals are held to ensure the ongoing fertility of crops and women. In the past a goat would be slaughtered and roasted. Different communities have their own customary practices to celebrate important moments in the agricultural year. Some farmers place a special pot, with an opening at the back, in their fields where small gifts are offered as tribute to the god of the particular field. Before harvesttime there

These thankful villagers are celebrating a bountiful harvest.

are many festivals that involve children dressed up with face masks, dancing in a field, to keep animals and birds out of the plots where they might eat the ripe seeds from the crop in damaging amounts.

FUNERALS

Sad events such as the death of a relative or a friend are considered festive occasions. They provide the occasion for the most important ceremonies of the forest foraging groups (Baka, Kola, and Medzan). On the morning of a funeral is the burial, which is a formal event and a show of respect for the relatives of the deceased. The afternoon may be devoted to a community affair that includes the family of the deceased. Family members will gather, each person bringing a supply of palm wine that is mixed together in one large *mimbo* pot. Participants then drink from this communal stock as a way of affirming their oneness, both in honor of the deceased and in acknowledgment that life goes on. In traditional African religion, which influences and even underlies Christian dogma on the African continent, there is a close affinity between

For centuries the grassland areas of Cameroon were divided into a lush mosaic of small kingdoms, each king having his territory administered by a number of fons or chiefs. No longer a formal part of governmental structure, chiefs nevertheless continue to play important roles in many rural communities. This is shown by the glamour that characterizes the initiation of a new chief. Special ceremonies, laid down by ancient custom, are organized and strictly followed. For example, Lake Oku has long been considered sacred. When a new chief was crowned, or enstooled, he was solemnly bathed in the lake's water. An enstoolment, which comes from the symbolic importance of a specially carved seat on which only the king can sit, is a major occasion, marked by large feasts, dramatic dances using traditional clan dress and masks, and a band performance to provide music for the joyful dances that follow.

the recently dead and the living. A funeral is not regarded as the terminal point of one's life, and this helps explain the festive air that characterizes the afternoon's activities. If the deceased person had a relative or friend who is in a dance society, the funeral will be enlivened by their performance. An elaborate funeral celebration can last up to three days, and the dancing often goes on throughout the night. Approximately a year later, lavish death services honor the deceased, who has then become an ancestor.

FANTASIA

Fantasia is an annual traditional celebration that takes place in northern Cameroon. It can also be celebrated anytime to mark a special occasion, such as a visit to the village of an important person. Visual images of fantasia that are displayed on tourist brochures give the impression that it is a horse race, but it is more of a parade, not a competitive event. Hundreds of horses often take part, and they and their riders are all are attired in bright and colorful costumes. The whole event is a communal celebration and a prime occasion for music and dance.

THE LELA FESTIVAL

The Lela festival is celebrated annually by the Bali people of western Cameroon. Lasting four days, the festival is held in December. Similar to all local festivals, the Lela festival is an important event for all members of the community, and Bali people who live and work away from home will make a special effort to return home to join in the festivities. It is a time for families to be reunited and old friends to renew loyalties. The village chief is the focus of attention all during the festival. On the first day he rides on horseback to the local river, followed by all the villagers. A cock is then sacrificed and examined by diviners. All being well, the diviners will confirm that the spirits are pleased and the parties can begin. The following days are filled with dancing, feasts, and the firing of guns in celebration. Everyone wears their very best clothes.

URBAN FESTIVALS

Festivals are as popular in towns as they are in the countryside. In the cities there is a blend of traditional forms of entertainment with modern Western practices. For example, among the more well off, cocktail parties are often given in their homes.

Just as a village festival takes place in the open space of a compound and involves the whole community, a town festival also becomes a public event. An individual who has been personally invited to a celebration by a host family feels free to invite someone else to come along, and the added guest may not even have a chance to meet the host during the party. This degree of comfortable informality applies to most social events at a public level.

FOOD

Cameroonian children tending to a stall in a rural market in Nyasoso.

>THE MAJORITY OF CAMEROONIANS grow most of the food they eat. There are regional differences in the variety of foods because changes in climate affect the kinds of crops and vegetables that can be grown.

In the south, where rainfall is regular, cassava, plantains, yams, and other root vegetables are staples in daily meals. In the north the temperature and rainfall are more suitable for the cultivation of corn, sorghum, and millet. The one common food feature throughout the country are sauces made from peanut paste and palm oil to add taste and flavor to what otherwise would be bland dishes.

An urban family enjoying a cooling drink together.

Cameroon's food choices vary from region to region. Fish and shrimp are featured mainly on the coast. Beef and poultry are considered delicacies. Vegetables are plentiful everywhere and are usually accompanied by a spicy sauce. The Cameroonian diet is characterized by starchy foods as staples. Corn is the most widely cultivated grain and is a staple in the Cameroonian diet.

123

A woman preparing cassava for cooking. Cassava originated from South America and is one of the most common vegetables found across West Africa.

VEGETABLES

CASSAVA is shaped like a carrot, with a brown skin and white flesh. The large tubers are boiled and then pounded into a white paste or dried as flour. Sometimes cassava is mixed with other vegetables and meat to make a stew. The leaves of the plant are also eaten, often in zesty sauces.

YAMS are easy to grow if there is sufficient rainfall. Yams are a basic food in many people's diets across all of Africa. The tubers are pounded like cassava and eaten in a variety of ways. (In the West, what are called yams are usually sweet potatoes, a different plant.)

COCOYAMS are prepared and eaten in much the same way as yams. They are tastier than yams and not as bland. Cocoyams, also called taro, grow vigorously in areas of heavy rainfall, such as the tropical rain forest region of Cameroon.

OKRA is commonly used in soups and stews because the pods have a thickening effect when cooked. Another name for this vegetable is gumbo.

GRAINS

SORGHUM is a family of valuable cornlike grasses that can withstand periods of drought. Sorghum grows up to 13 feet (4 m) tall. The lighter-colored sorghum grasses are eaten, whereas the darker ones are fermented to make beer.

MILLET, a name given to a group of grain grasses that produce small seeds, thrives in poor soil, and is able to survive drought and intense heat. Millet is used to make porridge, as well as beer, and is pale yellow in color.

Selling various grains, starchy cereals used in food, in a local market.

Grilled seafood is a popular snack and a good source of protein. It is usually sold near the docks.

CORN is commonly known in Cameroon as maize. Unlike other grains, which came from Asia, corn originated in Central and South America. When the grain is pounded and treated with lime, it produces cornstarch, called corn flour. The young heads of the plant provide sweet corn. Cornmeal, coarsely pounded without additives, is used in various dishes, such as boiled porridge.

MEALS

A typical Cameroonian breakfast consists of cornmeal porridge with bread and tea. A meal at lunchtime may have rice with fried plantains or a large omelet, and an evening meal could be boiled yams served with fish or meat, or cooked yams mashed with eggs and eaten with fresh vegetables. Beef, chicken, and liver are popular choices when a family can afford to buy meat. Venison, which is more expensive compared with other meats, tends to be eaten only by well-to-do people or at meals marking special occasions. Monkeys, dogs, and cats are sometimes hunted for their meat, too. Chicken mixed with peanuts and stewed with peppers and onions is a popular family dish.

The most common meal consists of *fufu*, a dumplinglike dough made from pounded corn, cassava, or yams, and *jammu-jammu* (JAH-moo-JAH-moo), a thick stew made from leaves of a local vegetable that resembles spinach, with spices and, occasionally, small pieces of meat. After pounding, the *fufu* is usually boiled until it becomes doughlike and is then placed in an enamel serving dish. The diners have individual plates or bowls of *jammu-jammu*. Small amounts of the *fufu* are taken by hand from the communal dish and dipped in the bowl of *jammu-jammu*. Main meals are most often eaten with boiled rice, yams, or plantains. Flavor is added to many dishes by seasoning with local spices and herbs.

- *If using your hand, use your right hand only.*
- *If fufu is served, break off a piece before dipping it into the soup or stew.*
- *Visitors will be offered food first, but when a guest, be sure not to eat more than a fair share of what is on the table.*
- *In traditional homes, men eat first, then women, and then children.*
- *If a bowl of water is passed around after the meal, rinse your fingers in it.*

Special dishes are reserved for important occasions. Among the Bali people, *shu-a* (SHOO-r) is made with a mixture of pounded peanuts and flour, which is then fried. During a wedding feast the paste is stirred with water to prepare a drink for the bridegroom and bride.

Chai-khana (CHAI-kah-nah) is a teahouse, usually set up in a taxi stand or bus station. Mobile *chai-khanas* are also common in Cameroon. The vendor will carry two buckets, one of hot water and the other filled with mugs and a large kettle. The tea is brewed from cloves and heavily sweetened with sugar. Although cocoa and coffee are also produced in Cameroon, they are seldom drunk there. Apart from tea, the most common hot drink is Ovaltine, a nutritious chocolate-malt powder mixed with milk or hot water.

COOKING MEALS

In the countryside cooking is done over a makeshift stove that consists of a small pile of charcoal between a few stones. Although traditional clay pots can still be found, more families nowadays use aluminum pots. A local stream is often used for washing dishes.

In cities and larger towns many families have electric or gas stoves and running water. In rural settlements people depend on the village well for fresh water. More villages now have a system to carry water from the well into the village.

A grain store is built to keep food fresh for long periods. Its floor is usually kept above the ground to deter insects and animals from reaching the food.

A pounder, or large pestle, is the most common kitchen implement in both the countryside and in towns because it is essential for the making of *fufu*. After the yam or other vegetable is cooked, it is mixed with water and pounded into a dough that is shaped as a soft ball.

STORED FOOD

The need to store food is more important in northern Cameroon than the south. In the southern forest regions, where rainfall is reliable, many crops can be grown throughout most of the year. In the drier climate of the north, farmers cannot always take the rain for granted, because some years will have a long dry season followed by a short wet one, thereby reducing the quantity and quality of the harvest. Many villages have a common storage area where surplus food such as yams will survive for most of a year.

Even when enough food has been grown to feed the entire family, canned food is sometimes bought at the market to add variety to the menu or when there is a special occasion. Canned sardines are a favorite among many Cameroonians.

A common sight at bus stations, and sometimes at makeshift stalls beside a main road, is a woman selling fruit or vegetables. This is usually surplus food grown by her family. Selling this fresh produce adds cash to the family pocketbook.

DRINKS

Most Cameroonians prefer to drink tea than coffee. Their favorite tea-drinking places are *chai-khanas*, local teahouses that also serve as meeting places for friends to exchange news and gossip. Besides teahouses, a common sight across Cameroon is a large truck making its way by road to remote villages to unload crates of soft drinks and Cameroon-brewed beer at local bars.

Palm wine is a popular alcoholic drink because it is locally made and inexpensive. A farmer may keep dozens of palm trees, planted at different times, so that there is a dependable supply of sap available year-round. A small cut is made in the trunk, and the sap is collected in a hollowed-out tube made from bamboo that is specially shaped to fit closely into the incision. This way not a drop of the sap is wasted before it is poured into a large calabash, where fermentation soon starts.

A vendor tending a small street stall selling homemade ice cream and sweets in Yaoundé.

HISTORY OF CAMEROONIAN FOOD

Many staples of the modern Cameroonian diet first came with the explorers of the New World of the Americas, sailing in a great Atlantic circle from Europe. The Portuguese brought in such staples as corn, cassava, and tomatoes. Other Europeans soon settled on the Cameroon coast, and their influence is reflected in the foods eaten today. For example, the French introduced omelets and French bread, and the English started the concept of desserts. For the most part, though, Cameroonians continue to prepare and enjoy their own traditional foods.

Foreign restaurants are found in the larger towns and cities. In 2004 Doula featured Greek, Lebanese, Italian, German, Japanese, and Chinese restaurants, a number of Parisian-style cafés, as well as small eateries offering pizza and hamburgers. Yaoundé, the capital city, offers a variety of cuisines, including Chinese, French, Italian, Russian, and Cameroonian. In the smaller cities street vendors and restaurants serve more traditional foods than foreign-inspired dishes.

SUYA (SOO-YA)

This is a traditional meat dish, served with rice. Serves four.

Ingredients

2 pounds (907 g) round steak

2 cloves garlic, crushed or finely chopped

1 teaspoon (15 ml) sugar

1 teaspoon (15 ml) dried ginger, ground

1 teaspoon (15 ml) cinnamon, ground

1 teaspoon (15 ml) chili powder

1 cup (250 ml) roasted peanuts, shelled, peeled, and crushed

Soak wooden skewers in water for 30 minutes. Remove any fat, then cut the steak into small bite-size pieces and place in a medium-sized bowl. Mix sugar, garlic, ginger, cinnamon, and chili in a bowl, then add the crushed peanuts. Sprinkle the mixture on the steak and mix thoroughly so every bite of the meat is seasoned. Thread onto the wooden skewers, close together. Cover and let marinate in the refrigerator for 30 minutes. Grill or barbecue the meat, taking care not to burn or overcook. Serve with rice.

AFRICAN CRÊPES

This is a traditional Cameroonian recipe for a thin pancake that uses mashed bananas in the batter. Serves four.

Ingredients

1¾ cups (430 ml) all-purpose flour

¼ cup (60 ml) granulated sugar

2 tablespoons (30 ml) confectioners' sugar

12 ounces (355 ml) milk

4 large ripe bananas, mashed

Pinch of salt to taste

Peanut oil for frying

Mix the flour, granulated sugar, and salt in a bowl and whisk in the milk, a little at time, making a smooth thin batter. Add the mashed bananas and stir to blend thoroughly. Heat a little oil in a small frying pan over medium-high heat, and then add about ¼ cup (100 ml) of the batter. Spread this with the back of a spoon or ladle so that it forms a thin layer. Cook for about 2 minutes, flip, and cook for 2 minutes more. Roll tightly, dust with the confectioners' sugar, and serve hot.

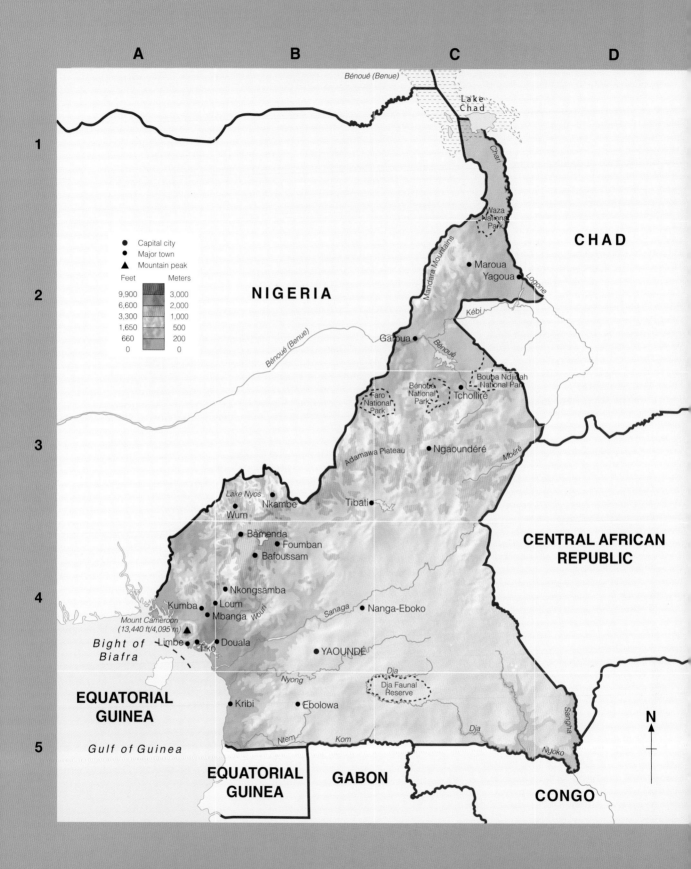

MAP OF CAMEROON

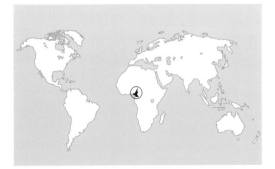

133

ECONOMIC CAMEROON

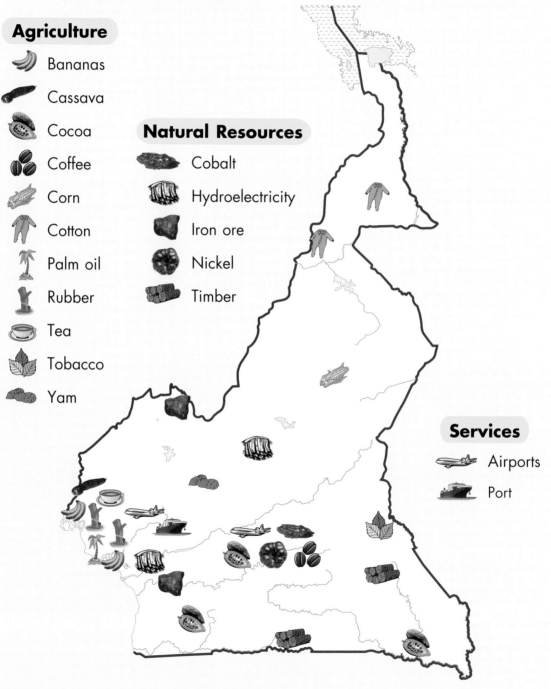

Agriculture
- Bananas
- Cassava
- Cocoa
- Coffee
- Corn
- Cotton
- Palm oil
- Rubber
- Tea
- Tobacco
- Yam

Natural Resources
- Cobalt
- Hydroelectricity
- Iron ore
- Nickel
- Timber

Services
- Airports
- Port

ABOUT THE ECONOMY

OVERVIEW

The Cameroonian economy is primarily agricultural with the main commercial crops being cacao, coffee, tobacco, bananas, and cotton. Petroleum products make up more than half of all exports. The economy suffered in the 1980s with a fall in the prices of coffee, cacao, and oil. The rising prices of oil and coffee, combined with the increase of all exports because of the implementation of structural reforms and prudent spending, have propelled the growth of the economy since 1995. Timber is also a major export, and reforms in the troubled forestry sector have been put in place with the aim of increasing sustainability and productivity.

GROSS DOMESTIC PRODUCT (GDP)

$42.55 billion (2009 estimate)

GDP PER CAPITA

$2,300 per capita (2009 estimate)

GROWTH RATE

-1.5 percent (2009 estimate)

CURRENCY

Communauté Financière Africaine franc (CFAF)
100 centimes = 1 CFA franc
US$1 = 470.32 CFA francs (November 2010)

LABOR FORCE

7.313 million (2009 estimate)

MAIN EXPORTS

Cacao, coffee, cotton, bananas, tea, rubber, palm oil, aluminum, timber, peanuts, crude oil and petroleum products

MAIN IMPORTS

Machinery, electrical equipment, transportation equipment, fuel, food, industrial and household goods, fertilizers, pesticides

TOURISM

185,000 visitors (2008)

MAIN TRADE PARTNERS

France, Germany, Japan, Italy, United Kingdom, Spain, Holland, United States

AGRICULTURAL PRODUCTS

Cocoa, coffee, bananas, cotton, palm oil, peanuts, corn, rubber, sorghum, sweet potatoes, yams, cassava, rice, millet, tobacco, cotton

NATURAL RESOURCES

Bauxite, iron ore, gold, oil, natural gas, timber

CULTURAL CAMEROON

Waza National Park
Founded in 1934 as a hunting reserve, Waza became a National Park in 1968, and a UNESCO biosphere reserve in 1979. Waza is home to lions, elephants, hyenas, Western giraffes, ostriches, antelopes, wart hogs, red-fronted gazelle, and 379 species of birds.

Maroua
This is Cameroon's northernmost major town, it is the starting point for exploring Manadara Mountains and Parc National de Waza.

Tabaski Festival
During Tabaski horse races and parades mark the end of Ramadan.

Foumban
The Grande Marché is a warren of narrow market stalls. The Grande Mosqueé faces the Palace of The Sultan which contains the Royal Museum. It is also a center for Cameroonian handicrafts.

Bafut Botanic Garden & Bafut Fon's Palace
A major tourist attraction and listed in The Worlds Monuments Watch of the 100 most endangered sites since 2006. The original palace was built of wood but was burned down by the Germans in the Bafut Wars and then rebuilt between 1907 and 1910 with help from the Germans after signing the peace treaty. The palace at Njibujang is also within this area and houses the tomb of the 8th King of Bafut, Achirimbi I.

Mfou National Park
This national park is where the CWAF runs its gorilla and chimpanzee rehabilitation project.

Lobeke National Park
Created in 2001, the park covers an area of 538,329 acres (217,854 hectares). Lobeke is home to some of the highest densities of forest animals in the Congo basin. There is an estimated population of 2,000 elephants and 3,000 gorillas. More than 62 different fish species are found in water in the area, 335 bird species, and thousands of African grey parrots.

Nki National Park
The park covers an area of 764,458 acres (309,365 hectares) and is largely hilly and inaccessible. The most sighted animals in this park are elephants, gorillas and buffaloes. There has been an increase in elephants from 1,547 in 1998 to 3,000 in 2006. The population of gorillas is estimated at 6,000 adult individuals.

Kribi
Cameroon's most popular beach resort.

Chutes De La Lobé
This set of waterfalls empty into a pool by the sea. It is located 5 miles (8km) from Kribi.

Boumba Bek National Park
The park is rich in wildlife species, notably forest buffaloes. It covers an area of 588,741 acres (238,255 hectares). It was gazetted as a national park in 2005.

ABOUT THE CULTURE

OFFICIAL NAME
Republic of Cameroon

CAPITAL
Yaoundé

AREA
184,000 square miles (475,440 square km)

POPULATION
19,406,100 inhabitants (Jan 2010)

MAJOR CITIES
Yaoundé, Limbé, Douala, Bamenda, Bafoussam, Maroua

OFFICIAL LANGUAGES
French and English

ETHNIC GROUPS
Cameroon Highlanders 31 percent, Equatorial Bantu 19 percent, Kirdi 11 percent, Fulani 10 percent, Northwestern Bantu 8 percent, Eastern Nigritic 7 percent, other African 13 percent, non-Africans less than 1 percent.

MAJOR RELIGIONS
Traditional beliefs 40 percent, Christianity 40 percent, Islam 20 percent

BIRTHRATE
34.1 births per 1,000 population (2009 estimate)

DEATH RATE
12.2 deaths per 1,000 population (2009 estimate)

INFANT MORTALITY RATE
63.34 deaths per 1,000 live births (2009 estimate)

FERTILITY RATE
4.33 children born per woman (2009 estimate)

LIFE EXPECTANCY
Total population: 53.69 years (2009 estimate)
Male: 52.89 years
Female: 54.52 years

PROMINENT CAMEROONIANS
Francis Bebey (musician), Manu Dibango (musician), Mongo Beti (writer), Ferdinand Oyono (writer), Samuel Eto'o (soccer player)

HOLIDAYS
National Day (May 20)
Independence Day (January 1)

TIME LINE

IN CAMEROON	IN THE WORLD

200–100 B.C.
Bantu tribes arrive from Nigeria.

1520
Portuguese set up sugar plantations and launch the slave trade.

1206–1368
Genghis Khan unifies the Mongols and starts conquest of the world. At its height, the Mongol Empire under Kublai Khan stretches from China to Persia and parts of Europe and Russia.

1600s
The Dutch take over the slave trade from the Portuguese.

1776
U.S. Declaration of Independence

1789–99
The French Revolution

1884
Germans set up protectorate over Cameroon.

1914
World War I begins.

1916
British and French troops drive Germans out of Cameroon.

1919
The London Declaration divides Cameroon into a British administrative zone and a French zone.

1939
World War II begins.

1945
The United States drops atomic bombs on Hiroshima and Nagasaki, Japan. World War II ends.

1958
French Cameroon granted self-government. Ahmadou Ahidjo becomes prime minister.

1960
French Cameroon granted independence and becomes the Republic of Cameroon with Ahidjo as president.

1972
Cameroon becomes a unitary state and is renamed the United Republic of Cameroon.

1982
Prime Minister Paul Biya succeeds Ahidjo as president.

1984
Biya elected to his first full term as president. The country's name is changed to the Republic of Cameroon.

IN CAMEROON	IN THE WORLD
1992	
Biya reelected in Cameroon's first multiparty presidential election.	
1997	**1997**
Biya's party, the Cameroon National Democratic Movement, wins a majority of seats in parliament amid allegations of irregularities. Biya is reelected president.	Hong Kong is returned to China.
1998	
Cameroon rated as the most corrupt country in the world by business monitor Transparency International.	
	2001
2002	Terrorists crash planes into New York, Washington D.C., and Pennsylvania.
Sovereignty of oil-rich Bakassi Peninsula is granted to Cameroon in an International Court of Justice (ICJ) ruling.	
2003	**2003**
Nigeria hands over 32 villages to Cameroon as part of the 2002 ICJ border deal.	War in Iraq begins.
2004	**2004**
Nigeria fails to meet deadline to hand over Bakassi Peninsula. Bija reelected president.	Eleven Asian countries hit by giant tsunami, killing at least 225,000 people.
	2005
	Hurricane Katrina devastates the Gulf Coast of the United States.
2006	
Nigeria withdraws troops from Bakassi Peninsula after a UN-mediated summit.	
2007	
President Biya's party retains a majority in parliament in the legislative elections. Nigerian senate rejects Nigeria-Cameroon agreement for handover of Bakassi Peninsula to Cameroon.	
2008	**2008**
Nigeria hands over Bakassi Peninsula to Cameroon, bringing an end to the volatile territorial dispute.	Earthquake in Sichuan, China, kills 67,000 people.
	2009
	Outbreak of flu virus H1N1 around the world.

GLOSSARY

Anglophile
A person fond of English ways.

bush taxi
A cheap means of public transportation using cars, minibuses, and small trucks.

calabash
A large gourd, dried and used as a container, often carved and decorated.

camaroes **(CA-mah-row-es)**
A Portuguese word for prawns or shrimp. The source of the name Cameroon.

chai-khana **(CHAI-kah-nah)**
A teahouse set up in a taxi or bus station.

cinder (breeze) blocks
Lightweight building blocks made with charcoal ashes (breeze) mixed with cement and sand.

enstoolment
The coronation ceremony of a new chief. The seat of power is a beautifully carved stool.

fon **(FOND)**
A local chief or king.

A *fondom*
A hereditary chiefdom.

Frananglais
Informal language made up of a mixture of French, English, and Creole words.

Francophile
A person enamored of French culture.

fufu **(PHU-phu)**
A doughy dumpling made from pounded corn or yam flour.

jammu-jammu **(JAH-moo-JAH-moo)**
A thick stew made from leaves of a vegetable similar to spinach.

jihad
Islamic term for a holy war.

mancala
A popular pan-African, two-player, strategy board game. Also called *warri* (WAR-ree) and *awele* (a-wee-LEE).

mimbo **(MEEM-boh)**
A clay pot with a thick rim to prevent spilling, used for holding water or oil.

pastoralists
People who live and work on farms, especially tending to animals.

pidgin English
A simplified version of spoken English used in Cameroon and elsewhere among speakers who do not share a common language.

Ramadan
The ninth month of the Muslim year, when devout Muslims fast between sunrise and sunset.

shu-a **(SHOO-r)**
A food of the Bali people, consisting of a pasty mixture made from pounded peanuts and flour, then fried.

FOR FURTHER INFORMATION

BOOKS

Homberger, Lorenz. *Cameroon: Art and Kings*. Seattle, WA: University of Washington Press, 2008.

Omatseye, Jim Nesin, and Omatseye Bridget Olirejere. *Going to school in Sub-Saharan Africa*. Westport, CT : Greenwood Press, 2008.

Sertori, Trisha. *First peoples of Africa : Baka of Cameroon, Samuru of Kenya, Tuareg of the Sahara*. South Yarra, Victoria : Macmillan Library, 2009.

FILMS

Greystoke: The Legend of Tarzan, Lord of the Apes. Directed by Hugh Hudson. The jungle scenes of Greystoke's upbringing by apes in "Equatorial West Africa" were filmed in the rain forest of what is now Korup National Park, in the Southwest Region of Cameroon. The waterfall featured in the film is Ekom Falls, south of Bafoussam, near the town of Melong. Warner Bros., 1984.

MUSIC

Dibango, Manu. *The Best of Manu Dibango*. Mercury Import, 2003.

Kaïssa. *Looking There*. Makai Records, 2005.

Nyolo, Sally. *Studio Cameroon*. Riverboat, 2006.

BIBLIOGRAPHY

BOOKS

Green, Malcolm. *Through the Year in West Africa*. London: Batsford, 1982.

Harris, Clin. *A Taste of West Africa*. London: Hove, 1994.

La Duke, Betty. *Africa: Women's Art, Women's Lives*. Trenton, NJ: Africa World Press, 1997.

WEBSITES

allAfrica.com: Cameroon. http://allafrica.com/cameroon/

BBC Country Profile: Cameroon. http://news.bbc.co.uk/2/hi/africa/country_profiles/1042937.stm

CIA World Factbook. https://www.cia.gov/library/publications/the-world-factbook/index.html

Encyclopaedia Britannica. www.britannica.com/bps/search?query=Cameroon&blacklist=90925

Fact Monster. www.factmonster.com/search?fr=fmtnh&query=cameroon&x=20&y=14

Infoplease. www.infoplease.com/search?q=cameroon&in=all&fr=iptn&x=32&y=10

MBendi Information: Cameroon—An Overview. www.mbendi.com/land/af/ca/p0005.htm

Nations Online: Cameroon—Country Profile. www.nationsonline.org/oneworld/cameroon.htm

INDEX

INDEX